WRITES OF LIFE

Using Personal Experience in Everything You Write

Robert Yehling

Open Books
PRESS

Published by Open Books Press, USA

www.OpenBooksPress.com
info@OpenBooksPress.com

An imprint of Pen & Publish, Inc.
www.PenandPublish.com
Bloomington, Indiana
(314) 827-6567

Print ISBN: 978-1-941799-29-1
eBook ISBN: 978-1-941799-30-7

LCCN: 2016907663

Printed on acid-free paper.

Cover Design: Min Gates

CONTENTS

ACKNOWLEDGMENTS

I'd like to thank the teachers, authors, editors and journalists who encouraged me to achieve excellence, relentlessly pursue facts and details, explore the stories within me, as well as my own heart and mind, and to stop for no one's label or definition of "limit."A few deserve extra thanks: Tom Robertson, Dr. Beverly Bosak, Dr. Don Eulert, Steve Scholfield, Bill Missett, George Salvador, Jim Kempton, Harvey Stanbrough, Gary Snyder, Charles Redner, Sheila Bender, Penny Porter, Michael Steven Gregory and Wes Albers from the Southern California Writers Conference, and Lillian and Tony Todaro from the Greater Los Angeles Writers Society.

A big part of my walk in this writing life has been to take a Johnny Appleseed approach and pay the gifts forward. That would not have happened were it not for people such as Dr. Celia (Jayashree) Alvarez and Dr. Carol Gray, who brought me to Ananda College of Living Wisdom, a four-year school where I chaired the writing department for several years; Dr. Meg Files, head of Pima College's Extension Course program, in which I taught for years; Missy Feller, Melissa Oxford, and Andres Torres, whose gave me forums in their high school writing classes; and the many people who have hosted my workshops and presentations, too numerous to name but huge in my heart. You know who you are.

Special thanks to Open Books Press, to my editor, Jennifer Geist, and the man who acquired *Writes of Life*, Paul Burt; and to my wonderful literary agent and friend, Dana Newman. Also much obliged to Sharina Brothers for her initial editing work in the first edition.

Writes of Life is dedicated to you. May your stories inform your lives and bring wisdom, illumination, greater understanding and inspiration to others.

—Robert Yehling • Summer, 2016

ABOUT THE *WRITES OF LIFE* FORMAT

Writes of Life plumbs the greatest and richest story material we possess—our own experiences. Designed for writers of all ages, professions, abilities, genres and purposes, these 12 chapters meet you in the middle. Great discoveries await you.

This book formed from a "Writes of Life" workshop series I first developed in 2002 and taught for the next four years. As such, it reads in a very participatory way, and regularly invites you to engage with the content. Since I am a book and magazine editor, and writing coach (as well as a former high school track coach), you'll feel my encouragement and soft pushes. I have broken down each chapter to make it a process that, like a book itself, has a beginning, middle, and end. Or, you can turn to a chapter that pertains to a current writing challenge. Within each chapter are four specific sections:

- Opening commentary, discussing the concept and showing it in action.
- Apply & Integrate: A committed writing practice is as vital as your vocabulary and ideas. This section works within the chapters to help you build a dynamic, exciting and fun practice.
- Exercises: I have created chapter-specific exercises, all fun, shaped around your life experiences, and designed to draw out the best in your writing.
- Q&A Takeaway: Every good presentation leaves room for a question-and-answer session, right? In that spirit, each chapter closes with a few common (and not so common) questions, which I answer. Many of these were first asked in my workshops. After Chapter 6, please notice that the section is retitled, "Questions for Further Discovery." By then, we're into the "writing phase" of Writes of Life . . . and the answers could well be sitting on the business end of your pen or keyboard.

—R.Y.

INTRODUCTION

I walked into the professor's office behind a grove of eucalyptus trees at U.S. International University, a small liberal arts school in San Diego (now Alliant University). The campus was one of six that, until he was overthrown, the Shah of Iran utilized to educate young Iranian men in the American way Out of 3,000 students who attended while I was there, more than half were from Iran and other countries. Talk about hearing great stories!

Inside sat Dr. Don Eulert, and his long, graying hair, handlebar moustache, full eyebrows, beaded vest and cowboy boots. His face told quite a story: A frontiersman of words. He looked like a cross between a mad scientist and a cowboy, with a little Mark Twain thrown in. He once helped bring the Japanese poetic form, haiku, to the U.S. through *American Haiku,* which he co-founded in the early 1960s. He'd just written *Outposts: Letters from Buffalo Bill Cody to Annie Oakley,* a fact-based tome of poems, letters and essays. He came to be the most knowledgable man I've known the study of global religious, rites-of-passage, and social rituals, some as ancient as shamans telling stories in caves 30,000 years ago. All ritual arises from an experience and a story.

I also quickly realized something else: he just the independent study professor I wanted to fulfill my goal: to become a diverse prose writer. Quickly.

Dr. Eulert put down the newspaper feature articles I'd written and he'd assessed before accepting me into this unusual semester-long arrangement, which he reserved for students he knew wanted to be serious writers. He kicked his feet up on his desk, and asked me a simple question: "Who are your favorite authors?"

I was stumped (same as I am today); how do you choose? It's like asking *Taxi Driver* and *The Departed* director Marty Scorsese to name five directors that define his sphere of influence. I'd figured Dr. Eulert would ask about my writing, my experience as a 19-year-old, award-winning newspaper journalist, the book reviews I'd written, or the many famous people I'd met.

I gave it a whirl. "Michener. Leon Uris. Tolkien. Irving Stone. George Eliot . . ."

"What is your ultimate goal as a writer?"

"To write novels and non-fiction books that do something for people," I said. "Where they feel like they're part of the story."

He puffed on his pipe. "You're a good objective writer; you know journalism. But I want to deconstruct your writing—then you can bring the reader into your stories with you, let them feel the setting, *taste* your dialogue, recognize something about themselves in your words . . . have their own experiences."

I was hung up on his second sentence: *Deconstruct me?*

Dr. Eulert watched me compassion, wisdom, light from a wellspring tapped by those who have ventured within themselves. Maybe I was a crackerjack newspaper writer, but he had a writing sage's wisdom and I did not.

I took a deep breath. "OK, let's go for it," I said.

"You have to completely trust the process that follows. It will open you up to write stories in a way that touch souls as well as minds and imaginations."

"That's what I want." I wasn't yet convinced, but this man spoke to the part of myself that wanted to be a great writer. It was as prominent in my psyche as a bull's eye, and Dr. Eulert, who would (much) later become chair of the Alliant University Ph.D. program in Integrative Psychology, had no trouble picking it up.

He reached into his overstuffed bookshelves and pulled out seven titles. "We're going to write in a way you've never tried before, but before that, read and study these writers."

I looked at the titles: *Fear and Loathing in Las Vegas,* by Hunter S. Thompson. *Giles Goat Boy,* by John Barth. *Little Birds,* by Anais Nin. *Electric Kool Aid Acid Test,* by Tom Wolfe. *On The Road,* by Jack Kerouac. *The White Album,* by Joan Didion. An anthology of Native American stories and poems. And a poetry book I'd first read in high school, *Turtle Island* by Gary Snyder. I had seen, and loved, Thompson's and Wolfe's work in *Rolling Stone,* which every self-respecting young male gobbled up religiously in the 1970s. I did not know the other authors, though

Kerouac and his "stream of consciousness" approach would soon become my favorite means of finding and brainstorming stories.

It was all there: Fiction. Non-fiction. "New Journalism" (the forerunner of Creative Journalism, Immersive Journalism, etc.) Erotica. Humor. Social, political, and spiritual issues. Deep, incisive observation. Tremendous plotting. Brilliant characterization. Varied states of being. All great writing, beyond my reach. But not my potential.

During our writing sessions, Dr. Eulert unleashed torrents within me. He said that to write well, one must be willing to walk different, often more difficult paths, meet the Muse wherever she might appear, open up to any and all experience—and *feel it*—and be prepared for whatever happened next. Even if it meant moving in an entirely different direction. A very shamanistic approach.

As I read these books, my conception of journalism and writing came crashing down. I studied voices, outlined plots, and watched these authors take an outside subject, connect to it, and reach deeply within themselves to embed the narrative with their perceptions, feelings, and realizations. They did this with headline-grabbing material. They also launched from very basic moments, which taught me something: *Our most mundane experiences and daily events can become magic through the power of story.* These authors told the story and were part of it at the same time.

My ways of observing life and people transformed. I listened intently not only to what people said, but also to the language beneath the words, behind their eyes, within their facial expressions. Since my minor was in psychology, that was probably a good thing. I looked for similes and metaphors in everyday life, then brought them to the page. I wrote "page after page after page of absolute drivel," to quote one of my favorite rock music writers, *Creem* editor Lester Bangs (later memorialized by the late Philip Seymour Hoffman in fellow San Diego music writer Cameron Crowe's *Almost Famous*). I broke through barriers. Once in awhile, a golden sentence or paragraph resulted. Hemingway's harsh self-analysis suddenly made sense: "I sit down each day hoping to write one great sentence."

In short, I began utilizing personal experience within much of what I wrote.

Nearly 30 years later, in 2008, the Institute for Dynamic Educational Advancement (IDEA) commissioned me to put together *Poetry Through The Ages,* a book-length website, designed like a curated museum exhibit. *Poetry Through The Ages* traced the 5,500-year history of Western poetry (originating, as far as I could find, with Sumerian princess Enheduanna's praise-poems about the goddess Inanna, written on cuneiform tablets). I wrote period and cultural histories, picked 20 classic poetic forms, and broke down their most famous *auteurs* and how the form evolved. The website concluded with the poetry curricula I wrote for grades 1 through 12, plus undergraduate and MFA-level studies.

One of my chosen forms was haiku, the pristine three-line word-moment. Zen on the page. As I researched how haiku migrated from Japan to the U.S., a name from my past zipped across my screen: Dr. Don Eulert. The professor who changed my writing life.

I made contact, and paid Don a visit at his Frog Farm ranch in eastern San Diego County, this time with 30 years and several books under my belt. Not surprisingly, we hit it off. One thing led to another, and in early 2011, I published some of Don's work in *The Hummingbird Review,* a literary anthology I edit, and invited him to be our featured reader at our launch event. Later, while teaching college in the Sierra Nevada foothills, I walked next door to visit iconic poet, conservationist and Beat writer Gary Snyder, whose *Turtle Island* won the Pulitzer Prize in 1975—and had been my favorite since high school. Gary asked who did the most to change my writing when I was young. What a great question! After I responded, he squinted with his owlish eyes that miss nothing. "Don Eulert . . . now there's a writer who lives what he writes. And vice-versa."

Such is the writing life. Such is the power of story. Nothing is more potentially powerful than the stories within us. Furthermore, we carry within us the capability of transmitting the essence of our life experience into every sentence we write. We can write a book of all our experiences, or a book or story with just one. We can pen thousands of words about an adventure, or drop one bejeweled sentence into a letter or essay that resonates with wisdom and experience. We can animate and empower otherwise fictional characters with our favorite sayings, hobbies, visions, with our likes or dislikes, with our greatest triumphs or most agonizing challenges. We can drop our experience into topical tales, telling what it feels like to parachute or base jump for the first time, or walking into an Alpine meadow rushing with the energy of fat snow-fed streams. We can take every thing we've ever known, every thing we've felt, every child or adult we held and kissed, every tear we've shed and every laugh we've unleashed, and utilize the raw energy, emotion and *presence* of these experiences. Our lives are our greatest minefields for writing material, and our journals the chemistry labs where we experiment and create.

Writes of Life coalesces four decades as an author, poet, journalist, essayist, and editor in a way that, I hope, inspires great leaps for you. The chapters challenge you to break limitations and reach into the deepest places, where both the best stories *and* their universal context life. This book is provocative, risky and perhaps even transformative. I have added two new chapters to the ten that comprised the original award-winning edition in 2006, as well as updating the exercises and narrative.

Most of all, *Writes of Life* is about having fun, perceiving new insights in yourself, expanding your writing horizons . . . and entertaining, educating, or touching others through your words. Or simply enriching your own life. We must be willing to access and mine our experiences, bruises, triumphs, failures, polished gems and rough stones, mix them together, and dive into places that hearts and minds often avoid. *Don't hold back.*

Ready to give yourself this gift and take this journey?

ONE

Our Life Experiences, Our Stories

Cultivating the fruits of our inner, outer, imaginative, spiritual and emotional lives to uncover ideas and stories.

"A great story always answers the questions we were about to ask."

—John Eastman

I stood in my garden with a handful of weeds and a shovel, drenched with sweat. My friend Steve, a prominent psychologist, helped me work the corn, spinach, tomatoes, lettuce, beans, peppers, squash, and a dozen types of herbs. We were close to the major harvest, from which five families would partake. The garden had reached its luscious, wildest self, where plants touch, intermingle, and grow through and around each other. It reminded me of the creative chaos that kicks up when stories and ideas swirl within us.

"You know," Steve said, "if you think about it, we're all as rich and diverse as your garden."

Leave it to a behavioral scientist to equate a vegetable garden with human character! I knelt down over a plot of hilled-up beans, drank from a water bottle to replenish the endless sweat with which I practically fed the garden, and asked him to elaborate.

He minced no words. "If you look inside yourself, if I look inside myself, there's the lover, murderer, giver, thief, sacred or holy man, divine mother-goddess, realist, dreamer, child, wanderer, worker, innovator, shaman-storyteller, enchantress, and every other archetype you can think of. We all have these, which is why people relate so well to the well-told personal story."

Great point! I was no stranger to the concept; I've perceived all along that I, like everyone else, carried the genetic seed of a family tree that stretches back 50,000 years or so—like all of our trees. But no one had put it to me so directly—or in a more enlivened, "this-is-you-right-now" way. It was like cramming 50,000 years of our heritage and legacy as human beings and putting it into *this present moment,* which of course is where we can do the most with it.

Years after Steve and I had this discussion in my garden, when I was teaching writing workshops in the U.S. and Europe and bringing up the various aspects of our inner selves, our afternoon came rushing back through a participant's question: "What would happen if I opened up all these things inside, and the things I've done in my life, and wrote about them?"

The short answer: You would tap the greatest source of material, stories, anecdotes and revelations available to any writer. You would tap your own experiences.

Imagine what would happen if we used our own experiences more in our writing. Imagine how those hard-to-write sections would leap off the page, buoyed by the infusion of knowledge, wisdom, and the *feeling* of having lived it. If you're writing a story or article about swimming in the ocean, what could be better or more engaging to the reader than sharing your favorite (or most harrowing) ocean swim in addition to the facts? Now, imagine slicing off one bit of your life story, or a single experience, and animating a fictional character with it. Suddenly, that character comes to life like a cartoon cel morphing into 3D, infused with a piece of your spirit, your access to the *character's* soul and purpose.

Good fiction and nonfiction writers dive deep into the nature of their characters or subjects—their deeper nature, concealed, dormant and ancient though it may be—and produce rich, expressive characters that drive stories. Sometimes, you get more than you bargained for—and you're willing to dive deeper into the subject matter. As a marathon runner, I thought I could write expertly about ultramarathon running. It's only a marathon plus added miles, right? Actually, the two worlds are quite different. Marathons occur on road courses; ultras usually take place on courses as daunting and borderline insane as the mileage itself. Ultra runners also tend to be obsessively determined, pain tolerant, focused, and fixated on their interests. By and large, they are highly successful people in their careers, some having achieved greatness and mastery. As one told me, "I'm addicted to adrenalin. I have to keep finding tougher challenges." This, while signing up for a 200-mile run through the Gunnison National Forest in

Colorado, the high country where there's more snow than oxygen (it seems) seven months a year.

Only when I paced a friend in the prestigious Western States 100-miler in California's Sierra Nevada mountains did I understand the ultra world better. I think these people are their own species, physically superior but maybe missing a gene called *moderation*, but that's beside the point. In a 26.2-mile marathon, I run for a little over three hours on a point-to-point road course. On the 35-mile Western States pacing leg with my friend, David Nichols, we ran, shuffled and hiked for eight hours overnight in the rugged Sierra Nevada canyons, climbing and descending 1,000 feet at a time, a geological rollercoaster. We ran with head lamps and flashlights over narrow trails, the light of the moon and occasional animal sounds our only companions for much of it. (If you want to bond with someone and create an instantly interdependent situation, pace them on an ultra. The two parties rely on each other completely.) Compare that to a marathon, in which everyone is tightly packed throughout (unless they are elite athletes).

When I finished pacing at 5 a.m., exhausted and starved, I realized I had just experienced the most remarkable and hardest run of my life, the one I would probably talk about more than all four of my Boston Marathons combined. Sure enough, a couple years later, here we are. And I was only a pacer.

I also had rich, powerful, life-affirming and fascinating story material. It sat right where it does today: in my muscles, cells, and psyche, always ready for another run on the page. I wrote about what ultras feel like, as well as sharing stories of the characters I met, every bit as eccentric as the musicians, surfers, astronauts, poets, healers, earth scientists, innovative doctors, and wanderers that have occupied portions of my professional life.

How does that look in full bloom? I offer Joyce Carol Oates as Exhibit A, B, and C. Joyce is an amazing one-woman writing machine, author of 75 books (including numerous *New York Times* bestsellers like *We Were The Mulvaneys*) and more than 1,000 published short stories and essays. At a book signing, she said, "When I write fiction, I'm not the voice of Joyce Carol Oates. But it starts right here."

She tapped her heart and her head. When I asked her to elaborate, she added, "If I can't connect my characters to an emotion

I've felt, and universalize it so that we all feel it when we read the book, then I haven't done my job."

A side note: more than half of Joyce's novels are either set in or reference upstate New York and the way the 1950s played out for teenagers. She grew up there, and was a teenager in the '50s. She spins the material over and over again, in different guises, through different characters, in different scenarios and plots. Her life *is* her literary taproot.

When we access what it means to be a human being, and what motivates and inspires them, we also tap into our potential to write from our own hidden treasures, pleasures or shadows. Know how TV crime dramas always point to the motive? There's a reason: motive drives decisions. It drives action. It also drives good writing.

Steve's comment took me for a ride that continues to this day. My life, and yours, is the repository of many thousands of stories, poems, tales, triumphs, failures, joys, woes, faces and places, discoveries and adventures. And we're accumulating more stories and material every minute. The more mindful of this we are, the more accessible our experiences become when we summon them. A quick ten-minute walk down 14th Street in New York City or Haight Street in San Francisco, or scanning a concert crowd or marathon starting line, brings me face to face with all sorts of potential stories. I connect to them through our shared experiences, sometimes as mundane as noticing an expression of frustration like my own when someone is trying to cross a congested intersection. As a friend commented when I was having trouble assimilating the jack hammers, honking horns, and overall sensory and noise overload after moving near Union Square in Manhattan, "Look at it this way: Two thousand fictional characters walk by you every 15 minutes."

It's all within us. Each of us carries the entirety of human nature. The tales that spring from our nature draw from the same sources that people have read, absorbed, listened to and studied since ancient yoga masters sang the Vedas in Sanskrit, or our deepest ancestors "told" their hunting/gathering stories with cave paintings. Personal stories form the basis of most great literature. The great 18th-19th century German Renaissance man, Johann

Wolfgang von Goethe, crystallized this deep universal truth: "Is not the core of nature in the heart of man?"

Our challenge is to contact, embrace and allow the magical, mystical storyteller within to spin our thousand and one tales with complete freedom and abandon. We're not chasing someone else's way; we're using our own walk as a most authentic foundation for our writing life. "Follow that will and that way which experience confirms to be your own," psychoanalyst Carl Jung wrote. This begins with a willingness to trust yourself implicitly so you can dive beyond the surface features of daily life and fully engage not only the five senses, but all twelve as taught in Waldorf Schools (life/well-being, touch, balance, movement, smell, taste, sight/vision, thought, speech/language, hearing, warmth/temperature, ego/the other; see Chapter Seven). By contacting and exploring our own depths, we tap into universal truth—which enables us to go deep into any person, character or life situation. Know how, when you're reading, the author will make a statement through narrative, or a character, that connects so personally that you say, "That's me!?" Those "A-ha!" moments can turn a story into a lesson, a piece of dialogue into words you'll never forget, a sentence into absolute magic. They grip the hearts of readers, and they don't stop turning the pages.

That's the goal, and it happens in exactly one way: by distilling our life experience, through our subject, onto the printed page. This combines two of my favorite adages: Socrates "Know thyself" and the eponymous "Write what you know." Add the two, and here's what you have: *Write what you know from within yourself.*

First, we must practice writing our own stories, becoming comfortable with spilling pieces of our lives onto paper. This is not egocentric, by any means. It vitalizes our ability to convey ourselves to readers.

Some writers start with journal entries. Others find it through that once sweeping, now waning mode of communication: letter writing. Many connect through poetry or songwriting. Others, through blogging or microblogging on social networks. Essays are perfect for this. So are short stories, vignettes, memoirs, and novels. The approaches are many, one of the beauties of writing and creativity. The key? Write and practice. Constantly. Try everything. Awaken that inner storyteller. Don't be concerned with anything at first but swinging open the floodgates and finding just how many stories you do have within yourself. The most ordinary moments can become quite extraordinary on paper. Former U.S. Poet Laureate Billy Collins has used this exact approach to sell hundreds of thousands of *poetry* books. "I tried writing deeper, archetypal and complex poems, but I couldn't even understand them myself. I'm not smart enough," he laughed one day when we compared our overly complicated early writings—my articles, his poems. Now, Billy draws out the magic in a moment, even something like sitting at a breakfast nook drinking coffee at 7 a.m., the most ordinary act imaginable. His readers respond to how he makes that nook part of their universe.

Ultimately, we want to reach the point where we can write about anything or anyone at anytime. Ever wonder how romance writers crank out so many books? Now you know: they plumb their hearts, their longings and desires, and infuse their characters—sometimes with fictionalized versions of their own romantic experiences.

I routinely use elements of my life when writing, whether direct experience (such as my forthcoming memoir, *Rooting*), or pieces of many very true stories woven into narrative or character form, with some identifying characteristics changed (such as I did in my novel, *Voices*). I opened *Just Add Water*, the biography I wrote about autistic surfing great Clay Marzo, with one of his surf sessions. Only I wasn't watching from shore, but bobbing on a surfboard next to him in the turquoise waters of Maui, where he lives. I grew up surfing, and know how tough it is. Clay's an acrobat, a magician on waves as big as 20 feet, what 1996 Olympic gymnastics gold medalist Shannon Miller described as "one of us, only on a board" when I showed her a YouTube clip of him. Meaning, she saw the world-class gymnast in this surfer. She connected through what she knew. I wrote Chapter One with all of this in mind, and from a point of view that made the prose dance a little sexier: in the water, with him. I tied my experience to Clay's session, but you'll never know it from reading the chapter.

We'll get more into disguising our experiences within our larger work, but a good example of this comes from the iconic movie *American Graffiti*. Director and co-writer George Lucas patterned three of the four male protagonists after aspects of his teen self—Terry the Toad (nerdy, but gets the girl), Curt Henderson (wants to leave the small town to chase his dream; Lucas grew up in a San Joaquin Valley agriculture community), and John Milner (street drag race champion; Lucas street-raced as a teen).

By incorporating your life experiences into your writing when the situation or story warrants, you write what you know best, and the writing tends to touch lives and create a life of its own. The research lies within you. Don't hold back; move forward and watch how your writing and storytelling blossoms. Let's go to work.

APPLY & INTEGRATE: Build Your Daily Practice

Writing is a magical, mysterious expression that many of us want to practice so badly, but invariably, one of those things "we'll get to." Yet, we wonder, "Why can't I write as richly as Joyce Carol Oates or Tim O'Brien? As passionately as Isabel Allende? Or emotionally rich and creepy as Stephenie Meyer? Trigger-happy with colorful dialogue, like Elmore Leonard or Chuck Klosterman? As prolifically as Stephen King, Louis L'Amour or Sue Grafton? As magically as J.K. Rowling or Richard Paul Evans? Or as beautifully and mystically, capturing the cosmos in the ordinary, as Annie Dillard, Anne Lamott or Louise Erdrich? Or Billy Collins?"

The simple and incorrect answer is *talent.* True, they all are loaded with it, but that's not the reason. Rather, these authors and most others will tell you, "I sat down every day and I wrote." There's the magic potion: deliberate practice. The key to becoming a prolific writer is to write every day, no matter what. Write about everything that entices, surrounds, consumes, empowers or ignites you. Write stories, letters, poems, dialogue you hear . . . everything. Great American author Henry Miller never wrote original material for more than four or five hours a day unless he was on deadline. When he died in 1981, he left behind 40 books, 1,800 original pieces of artwork, and more. How did he crank out that much material on four hours a day? He wrote *every day.*

A few simple tips to build your daily practice:

- **Carve out your writing time.** Pick a time when you are most likely to be undisturbed. For some, it's the morning. For others, it's nighttime. Even if it's only 30 to 60 minutes at first, make it your sacred time. Guard it with your life.

- **Keep a journal.** Make the journal your sacred space for writing, discovering the beauty of the unfolding story or observation. Also make it a chemistry lab, experimenting with words, phrasing, dialogue, different formulas of putting your experiences into writing. Try to write in it daily, or at least several times per week.
- **Read good writing.** Start reading *as a writer:* How did the author draw you in? What phrases, metaphors, words or descriptions captured you? *Listen* to the dialogue of each character, the voice inflections. What is sweeping you away? Or throwing you off? Write about it. Practice what you've read.
- **Be observant of everything and everyone.** Good writers are ever-absorbent sponges: Anything they observe or experience is potential story material.
- **Practice solitude.** Pray, meditate, observe nature, or walk silently in a meadow, shoreline, or forest. Use this time to let the mind go . . . then bring in whatever you want to write. Solitude is the necessary companion for writing.
- **Write. Write. Write.**

EXERCISES

- Write out a life experience as completely as possible, in a 500-to 2,000-word piece. Consider the emotional, imaginative, spiritual and physical elements and its principal figures or characters (in addition to yourself). Shape it as an article, essay, short story, monologue, dialogue or travelogue.

- Every day for the next week, write a different story or vignette about an aspect of your life in your journal. Whether the piece is 100 or 1,000 words, give it a beginning, middle and end.

- What are your five greatest fantasies or flights of imagination? Write a paragraph about each.

Q&A TAKEAWAY

Q: How do I trust or open myself up to tell my life stories?

A: Simply allow yourself to tell the full story. I use a three-question approach: What happened? How it did affect me? What happened next? When you start to write, details and memories will return, sometimes flooding through. Every time you follow and write them out, you will open yourself up further.

Q: What is the difference between autobiography and memoir?

A: An autobiography is a chronological review of a life. A memoir focuses on a specific, life-changing event or experience, what led up to it, and how it impacted your life afterward.

Q: How do I know when I've tapped into an "A-ha!" moment of "universal truth"?

A: When you are connected to your writing, and your feelings, words and phrases will emerge that may give you goose bumps. Or, you'll think later, "did I really write that?" If you describe the raw, deep feeling and emotion, you'll tap into readers' emotions, feelings, and life experiences. You've tapped into universal truth.

Q: How do I "keep going" when the story becomes difficult, or when I reach an experience about which I want to write but can't seem to go any further?

A: First step: walk away from your paper or computer, take a walk, and make yourself busy for awhile. Muster up the courage to write that next sentence. Ask yourself, "What completes this story?" Take the most emotionally charged sentence from your last writing session, and build from that. Then write one sentence at a time. You can do it!

TWO

The Circle of Life

The many facets of our lives, interests, tendencies and personalities are accessible every moment: Dreams. Intuition. Presence. Observation. Senses. Imagination. Tap into your inner universe, our circle of life, and bringing out the jewels in ourselves.

"What each must seek in his life never was on land or sea."

—Joseph Campbell

How many times have we read a paragraph, sentence or dialogue exchange between characters and asked ourselves, "Where did *that* come from? They're telling my story!" The author dove so deeply with her narrative that it rattled our bones—not to mention transforming our perception of the piece itself. Did the author consciously create that amazing line of dialogue or metaphor? Did she know her audience so well that she *knew* you would sit straight up in your chair when reading that particular passage?

Likely not—though if you had such a stirring "A-ha!" moment, rest assured the author felt the words flow out a little more deeply, too. So then, how did it happen?

Technically, the author took one of many routes to create that memorable prose. Her process, however, followed a direct path: She trusted and allowed the creative process to carry fully her deep within her own story, and her inner self, into that rich place beyond intellectual consciousness—the Creative Dream, as the late, great novelist John Gardner termed it—where all things are possible and all stories can be told (see Chapter Three). She opened herself to the entirety of her experience and *did not hold back*—the unofficial mantra for this book, this type of writing, and really, any form of creative expression. Get used to seeing this phrase some more.

Question: what would happen if you sat down and wrote out everything you have ever done, perceived, observed, dreamt, read, said or heard in conversation, intuited or sensed? What if you applied that life experience, making it instantly available to access and use at any given moment? That would include everywhere you've traveled, every person you've met, every emotion you've expressed, every flight of fancy or imagination you've entertained and everything you've remembered. How many potential stories, anecdotes, vignettes, poems and songs are there? Can you even count that high? (Hint: look up at the sky on a clear summer night. That's what lies within you.) Can you picture how these pieces might branch into stories, and from there, twigs of vignettes and anecdotes, and leaves of figurative phrases that put together moments, images from your experience? Feels like the Big Bang igniting, doesn't it? Which is why the old adage, "We have a book within us," falls woefully short.

We can help ourselves immensely by understanding and accessing the galaxies of raw literary material within us. This is not rocket science or some outrageous theory of metaphysics. Rather, it's a matter of embracing and acknowledging the importance and larger significance of our lives and experiences, invoking our senses to be fully alert and present, putting our hearts and intellects together, and setting sail with our pens (and computers). In other words, time to take the the daily approach of any child at play. Once we depart, we may never again lack ideas or content in our writing. Wrote German poet and essayist Rainer Maria Rilke, "For the sake of a single verse, one must see many things, one must know the animals, one must feel how the birds fly and know the gesture with which the little flowers open in the morning. One must be able to think back to roads in unknown regions, to unexplained meetings and to partings one had long seen coming; to days of childhood that are still unexplained; to days in rooms withdrawn and quiet and to mornings by the sea, to the sea itself, to seas, to nights of travel that rushed along on high and flew with all the stars."

In one paragraph, he captured the journey on which we're embarking.

While teaching a "Writes of Life" session at a creativity conference in Tampa, I drew a circle on an easel to explain what feeds us—within and without—and how that integrates into our body and mind so that we can write from it. This is our "Circle of Life." We all have one, and trust me, it fills up fast once you dig in. Each segment represents the sum total of a particular quality. It includes:

- Memory: Intellectual, Cellular, Soul and Tribal
- Awareness
- Presence
- Intuition
- Receptivity
- Dreams
- Reading
- Solitude
- Sensory Perceptions
- Focus
- Conversations
- Journey/Landscape
- Heart Feelings/Passions
- Spirit/Inspiration
- Imagination

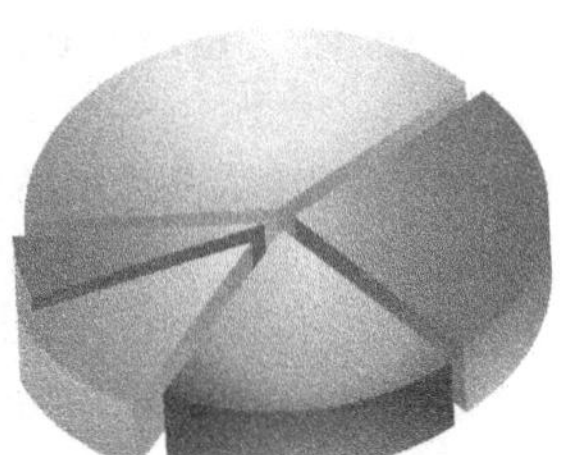

The center of this circle says: **Integration. Mindfulness. Presence. Next Word.**

The premise is simple: If all of these aspects of your life can come together and become your writing bedrock, then (along with incisive writing and a good story line or topic) they will enable you to produce great work that stirs the minds, hearts and souls of your readers. Each element stands on its own, as does hydrogen, oxygen, argon, etc. on the Periodic Table of the Elements. However, if you combine them and put them to work, you will feel like you have the universe behind you with every sentence, rather than scratching for something to write on that ever-imposing blank page or screen. The next word you write will be a new voyage of sorts, heading into unknown territory or waters; what's going to happen next? "What each must seek in his life never was on land or sea. It is something out of his own unique potentiality for experience, something that never has been and never could have been experienced by anyone else," said Joseph Campbell, who re-educated us on mythology in the latter half of the 20th century by inviting us to address the great myths as allegories for the myths and archetypes *within us*. Each of us has his or her own mythology, Campbell said. Just like each of us has a bedrock of writing material.

If *do not hold back* is our mantra, then *trust* is our motto. Trust in your ability to connect to these aspects of yourself, and in how you write them out. Trust your *voice* to carry you directly into whatever you write; no need to borrow from anyone else. We all have unique spoken and creative voices; the trick is to find them. Trust that whatever you decide to write has the potential to become a full expression of that moment, story, character or season. Trust that it will almost certainly lead you to another story or perception you thought was left well behind in childhood or adolescence. Most of all, trust that, at any moment, you can turn to your Circle of Life and draw from it *exactly* what you need at that moment.

Remember what I mentioned earlier about deliberate practice? That's the next step. Sit down, close your eyes, offer up a brief self-starting affirmation or inner prompt such as, "Bring me everything that relates to (topic of story)," and calmly *trust* what happens next. Become a receiver. Write down what follows; don't choke it off or edit it. By allowing apparently inconsequential phrases and thoughts to flow, you open the doors to the writing that captures exactly what you perceive, observe, think or feel.

Embrace your Circle of Life. If you write fiction, create Circles of Life for your characters. The Circle of Life is a great ally. It is also the most loyal. It is where every writer's inner Muse lives. If you work with this circle, it will return its bounty to you—a thousandfold.

ELEMENTS OF THE CIRCLE OF LIFE

- **Memory:** Memory is the most mysterious and intriguing aspect of the mind, the great basin that houses everything we've ever experienced, and how we experienced them. There are four principal types of memory: Intellectual, Cellular, Soul and Tribal (or Collective).

Intellectual memory consists of facts, snippets of conversation, observations, readings and physical experiences. A 2010 *Scientific American* article estimated that the human mind has an intellectual capacity of 2.5 petabytes—about 1 million gigabytes, or 1 million billion bytes. It sounds as big as a universe, but like the universe itself, that is only what can be "seen" or quantified. There's much more . . .

Cellular memory is what our body remembers, even if our mind blocks it out. Physical feats (and accidents), traumatic and heightened experiences, smells and sounds, injuries, and great adventures lodge in our bodies. It happens to all of us. Each cell has an intelligence of its own; each body has about six trillion cells. As Poet Li-Young Lee reminded me, there's a poem or story in every cell, just waiting for a pen to board for the ride onto the page.

Soul memory can also be called Ancestral or Genetic memory: The genetic and spiritual memory we bring into life. When I am in Germany or New England, I often feel like I'm a German writer/traveler, Italian coastal farmer, or Plymouth and Jamestown-based colonial leader. My ancestors were; I carry their DNA, their memory. This provides great access for historical fiction and nonfiction writers, who must write in a state of presence, as if the centuries-year-old scene is spreading out before their eyes, right now. Same goes for travelogue writers who dig into the history of their

Tribal (or Collective, or Primal) memory is the vast pool of experiences in which we've partaken in conjunction with our culture. It's also a memory of collective survival: The knowledge of lighting a fire when we're lost in the wilderness is an instinct borne by a primal memory. So is gathering around that fire to share a story; it dates back to our most ancient forbears, the shamans connecting hunter-gatherers to the mysterious "other side." When you write a good cultural story, the reader's tribal memory will be triggered.

Now, onto the other elements of the circle:

- **Awareness:** What is happening around you? Can you describe every sound, movement or color *right now?* Our lives are defined by the depth and acuity of our awareness. The more mindful we are of our every perception, observation, thought, feeling, emotion and place *in this moment*, the more vibrant and abundant our lives—and writing—become. Li-Young Lee says, "Live in super-conscious abundance." Bring full awareness into your life and writing.
- **Presence:** What is happening *right now?* Presence is the ability to forego past and future while remaining in the "eternal now." That's what it is: eternal, without beginning or end. While awareness is an active engagement, presence is settling into a state of being. Great writers lock into the present word, sentence or phrase, and stay there—for hours. Their stories reflect it. We'll concentrate on writing in a state of presence in Chapter Four.
- **Intuition:** Einstein famously declared that intuition was the most valuable asset a human being possessed. *Trust* your gut feeling, your intuition, your "sixth sense." Let it lead the way. Learn to attune to these messages, which cut through the busy world to inspire, warn, or enlighten you. If you receive such "out of the blue" direction when writing, *go where you're directed.* Intuition does not lie; it guides. It's a writer's best friend. As my friend Marty Balin, the rock & roll hall of famer, and founder of legendary psychedelic rock Jefferson Airplane who later wrote the 1970s #1 hit "Miracles" put it, "If something comes along and punches you in the gut, go with it. Write it down. It is the best thing that could possibly happen." Balin knows: the opening stanza to "Miracles" punched him in the gut while in India, he wrote it out in 45 minutes . . . and millions of radio plays and sales later, it remains one of the 50 most-played rock songs in history. Not bad for 45 minutes!
- **Receptivity:** We must be receptive to new ideas, concepts, experiences, discussions, people and, yes, intuition. Open yourself to be receptive to new developments—and write

about them. If something new happens, write about it in your journal. That will integrate the experience further. Today's receptivity might be tomorrow's chapter, character . . . or book.

- **Dreams:** Dreams are the rich, adventurous lives we lead when our bodies are sleeping. Fences are down, ideas are limitless, and everything is possible. It is the ideal writer's world. I once created for NASA a commemorative magazine for the 25th anniversary of Apollo 11 from a dream in which the Apollo 11 logo appeared. Now, from dreams, I regularly procure story or character ideas; the harvest ranges from a key sentence to an entire book. Dream structure is the same as narrative structure—you travel along a winding road with many tangents, some of which you venture down, but ultimately, the dream has a beginning, middle and end. Make your dreams a great contributor to your writing life. You'll often find pots of literary gold.
- **Reading:** When I was a teenaged journalist, a veteran writer told me, "Good writers read good writing." Reading and cross-reading (several books and genres simultaneously) are essential to the writing process; they help feed us with ideas and inspiration. They also help us expound and collect knowledge to amplify our ideas, and show us the zillion and one ways to create a story from the same starting point we all share: The first sentence. Study the nuances of language and how authors move the characters and narrative, or how they interview their subjects. When I am writing about someone, I always look at their home libraries, as well as DVD/video and CD collections, displayed works of art, furnishings, knick-knacks, and the contents of their garages and shelves (if I can gain access). It's a great way to know someone. Read, read, read . . . and not just books.
- **Solitude:** There is a famous yoga aphorism: "Solitude is the price of greatness." It's also the price of being a dedicated writer. Silence and alone time is not the way of our increasingly noisy and distracting world, but it must become *your way.* Your productivity will relate to your ability to create quiet space and be comfortable within it;

the inability to sit still and "hang in there" is a primary reason why millions of unfinished ideas lie in boxes and closets. *Writing Personal Essays* author and workshop teacher Sheila Bender says, "Solitude is a state in which a wide variety of feelings come to inform us about our lives and those of others we are concerned about. You can explore, take in, give out, breathe freely."

- **Senses:** We grew up learning about five senses—touch, taste, sight, hearing, smell. If you do nothing more than look at a life experience and trace it through each of these senses, then you'll likely produce a large essay. If you attended a Waldorf School, or have a child or grandchild that does, you know they teach 12 senses, as classified by famed Austrian educator and anthroposophist Rudolf Steiner. The other seven are a novelist's or creative non-fiction writer's Dream Team: Life/well-being, balance, movement, thought, speech/language, warmth/temperature, and ego/the other. In addition, Steiner regarded "sight" and "vision" as two sides of a coin: one is external, the other internal. We will discuss their particular writing applications and strategies of use in Chapter Seven.
- **Focus:** One of the great creative spirits of the 20th century, Mary Caroline Richards, cited the Latin root for *hearth,* or fireplace, when she described "focus." What happens when we sit in front of fires and they clutch our awareness? We're zeroed in on those burning logs. That's the focus we must bring to our writing—the sentence is the fire, and your entire being is the fuel. Nothing else matters. Editors can spot lack of focus instantly; the writer breaks off at a juicy, deep place and switches subjects—or backs out of the passage entirely. Make that full plunge and produce stories and characters that endure.
- **Conversations/Voice:** Our internal and external conversations build our spoken and written languages—including the idioms, idiosyncrasies, slang, colloquialisms and snippets of local dialect that season our essays, stories and characters. Also, the words between the lines, the unspoken words, which often carry far more meaning. The key to good conversation and its literary expression, dialogue (fiction) or quotes (non-fiction), is *attentive listening.* We

all carry the combination of our life experiences in the way we speak, too. For instance, my speaking voice mixes California surf-speak, Australian, Southern and British slang, the descriptiveness of a true lover of nature, a little southern twang (I use *y'all* and *fixin' to* much more than the average California bear), some closed-fist New York City pop, sports talk, corporate speak and cinematic verbiage. Pinpoint your *complete l*anguage—and listen for that of others. Languages are like snowflakes: no two are exactly alike. Voice brings an endless stream of language—and languages—into text.

- **Journey/Landscape:** Good writing is a journey for you and for the reader. How do you *feel* when you're on a journey? Convey it. Use action verbs to move the train forward. Study the landscape, the host of said journey. What natural formations move, inspire you, or emotionally charge you? I learn about a person's ideas, interests, inner languaging and sense (or lack) of adventurism, and even whether they're a feeling or thinking person, by asking one question: "What are your three favorite geologic formations?" Mountains, water, rivers, creeks, streams, brooks, bluffs, hills, crags, hollows, swamps, canyons, deltas, waterfalls, arroyos, canyons, mesas and grassy meadows reflect our inner and outer worlds. I love how Walt Whitman connected us to landscape in *Leaves of Grass:* "Were you thinking that those were the words, those upright lines, those curves, angles, dots! No, those are not the words. The substantial words are in the ground and sea, they are in the sea, they are in you." To paraphrase Gary Snyder, find what makes up your place in space.
- **Heart Feelings/Passions:** Great Southern novelist Eudora Welty wrote, "I like writing because writing is sexy. I like writing because writing makes me feel more deeply." What impassions you? What drives you crazy, wild, or deeper into your heart? Or the heart of another? Whatever makes your blood pump—whether in love or anger, in joy or sorrow—is a great writing subject. Combine action, expression and emotion in every scene if possible.
- **Spirit/Inspiration:** What beliefs and practices constitute your spiritual life? Your spiritual bedrock will (and

should) influence your perception of the world and others, and your writing. However, your walk should expand your writing, not constrict it. A perfect example is Anne Lamott, author of *Bird by Bird, Blue Shoe, Traveling Mercies,* and others. Anne is a born-again Christian unafraid to dig into life's more sordid side. Her works are steeped with compassion and forgiveness, deep truths of her inner life. She doesn't preach truth; *she lives and writes it.*

- **Imagination:** Mark Twain said, "You can't depend on your judgment when your imagination is out of focus." If intuition is the most vital cellular quality we possess for experiencing life and writing about it, then imagination is the most important mental quality. Without the ability to imagine, percolate ideas and go beyond the ordinary, we will be limited. Your imagination is a preview of your life's coming attractions.

Get to know these elements. They all exist within you.

APPLY & INTEGRATE

- Increase your daily journaling time to 30 minutes—even if you have to break it into two 15-minute sessions.

- Every day, write down an idea, person, character or situation about which you would like to write.

- Find a book completely different from your usual reading list. Study how the author pulls you into the story. Look for particular uses of observation, senses and life experiences. Try to connect your own experience to what you would read. Where would you take the story from there, using your own life?

- During the next week, go to a bookstore and read the first pages of 20 different books – including at least five memoirs. Feel and observe how the author grabs you. Use your own voice to "grab" your journal in the next entry.

- As you go about your day, observe and interact from a more detached perspective, asking yourself, "What's trying to happen here?" This will create greater mindfulness, clarity and presence as you hone the ability to write about anything and everything.

EXERCISES

- Take a spin on the Circle Life. For each segment described in this chapter, write down three specific things from your experience in this area. When finished, you should have a list of 36 items.
- Choose one of those items and write your experience, throwing down everything you can feel or remember. Forget about punctuation or tight structure; this is a brainstorm.
- Now see if you can connect two or three items together, merge them . . . and see what life experience pops out from that. Something will: every time we write down a life moment, it triggers others, like peeling layers of an onion. Write for 20 minutes.
- Take your list further. Continue adding to it as your mind awakens to the elements in the Circle of Life, and feeds you incessantly (which it will). For each item, write a couple of sentences to capture the essence of that moment, much as one would scratch out a couple of images in a dream notebook before trying to get back to sleep.
- If your lists and earlier writing lead you into a story or essay, or even a vignette or anecdote, see where it leads you. Chances are, this adventure will exceed your expectations—and venture far beyond the original thought, or moment, that you wrote on the Circle of Life.
- Always add to your Circle of Life. Make it your creative roadmap, to be visited frequently. It *always delivers on its promise!*

Q&A TAKEAWAY

Q: How do I sit down and "flick on the switch" so that aspects of myself integrate into my writing?

A: Write until you feel your words flowing, rather than thinking about structuring the perfect sentence. Work to get everything down you want to say. That mentality will engage your heart. Then, write what moves through you. Don't be afraid to use the pronoun "I."

Q: How can I summon specific memories at will when I'm writing?

A: Identify a memory, and write everything you can about it. Go back to it an hour later, and see what you can add. Then return a day later, and add what has "come to you" since first writing down that memory. Practice until your mind expects to be summoned. (This is also great practice for memory deficiency or recall challenges, by the way.)

Q: What is a good strategy for converting my personal experience into stories?

A: Take one experience and write all you can. Then another. Find the high points and dramatic points of that particular experience, what moved, changed, affected, or somehow shifted within you. Then write it out as a story, either narrating yourself or writing through characters. Then see if you can drop tidbits of story into a topic with which you have personal experience.

Q: How do I take a story or book idea into this Circle of Life and connect with the great storehouse of experience, wisdom and observation within me?

A: By moving your story, book idea or experience through all stations in the Circle of Life. Do this with several topics, skipping no steps, and don't be surprised at the volume of material you write. Soon, you'll be able to walk any idea on the Circle with your pen . . . and beyond that, you will be able to weed out or focus ideas based on any or all of the specific stations.

THREE

The Creative Dream

Journey to the junction of creativity, craft and intuition, where time stands still, ideas and stories flow freely, characters blossom, and concepts connect from every direction imaginable.

"Writing is the high alchemy of the soul that combines words and ideas to create magic."

—Sharif Khan, author, *Psychology of the Hero Soul*

Joyce Carol Oates is one of the most prolific writers in American literary history. She has written 75 books of fiction and short stories, including best-sellers such as *We Were The Mulvaneys,* exquisite character and societal studies like *Broke Heart Blues,* and the absorbing Blonde, her take on Marilyn Monroe's turbulent life.

While reading in New York City, Joyce often paused and stared beyond the fourth-floor window overlooking Union Square. Her deep-set eyes peered far into the night—or into a future story whirling through her ceaseless imagination.

Later, during the question and answer session, we engaged in a lively back-and-forth about the Creative Dream, the state of mind that writers, artists, and musicians covet when working:

Me: "What is your level of awareness while you're immersed in your writing?"

Joyce: "My entire world consists of the story I'm writing. Nothing else."

Me: "And the characters?"

Joyce: "They breathe and live through me. I record what they say."

Me: "How do you lend your voice to them, to your fiction writing?"

Joyce: "Joyce Carol Oates' voice does not appear in my fiction."

Think of the creative dream as a realm beyond the workaday world. It is a state of full immersion, detached rom daily routine and duties. In many ways, it is like a walking meditation, a turning within—only our "walk" takes place with words. In this place, our ideas, stories, characters and their voices take shape and flourish, often beyond our intentions, sometimes to our own astonishment. I can't tell you how many times I've finished a writing session, looked up 30 minutes later at the clock—and four hours have passed. Then, when I look at what I wrote, I always see something beyond what I'd considered writing. I don't even remember writing it; it just seemed to flow out in the course of the article or story blazing through me. When that happens, I know it has been a good session—and I want to return for more.

Virtually all fiction and creative non-fiction writers work in the Creative Dream regularly. All forms of writing benefit greatly from our ability to get quiet, give our calculating minds a rest, and let the subject of our writing, or our story, percolate and speak through us, *guide* us. It may sound strange, esoteric or a little otherworldly, but when you enter the Creative Dream, you enter a place of enhanced awareness, or superconsciousness, where everything is possible and nothing is limited. Like a sleeping dream. Afterwards, when I leave my desk and walk into the world, I feel alive, energized with a new purpose and creativity, like I've had a spiritual awakening or a rebirthing. Or a B-12 shot. In a sense, I have.

When authors discuss this state of creative mind, their remarks are creatively different—of course—but their points are the same. In his landmark book *The Art of Fiction,* late novelist John Gardner noted that immersing one's self in this boundless place of pure storytelling is essential to good writing. Author Gloria Naylor (*The Women of Brewster Place*) explained the process this way: "So much of what I do is unconscious. I choose not to direct why certain images appear when I'm writing. I just let them lead and take me where they will, and then I proceed to craft the language around it the best I know." Added Jyoti Arora, the author of *Dream's Sake and Lemon Girl,* "Creativity is a magic wand that works two ways. When you set it in action and seek to create something, it does not just brings into existence that object or work, it also raises in your heart a dream, a hope, and a will to achieve that creation. And when all else seems lost and steeped in hopelessness, the magic of creativity can still keep you going."

For some, like *Vampire Chronicles and Christ the Lord: Out of Egypt* author Anne Rice, the creative dream is precisely that—a state of dreaming tied to her work. "To me, daydreaming is intimately connected with writing. Writing is like daydreaming. *I*t's putting down in dramatic form whatever is on your mind," said Rice.

Anne's husband, the late poet Stan Rice, spoke years ago at a writer's conference I attended. When the subject invariably turned to his wife, a participant asked about her writing process, in a funny way: "What is it like being married to someone who writes vampire novels and absorbs herself like she does?"

Stan chuckled warmly and gave his answer a minute to form. "From Midnight to 8 a.m., Anne is not my wife," he said. "She goes into her office and becomes her characters, her stories. She's *gone.* I don't have any contact with her. She wouldn't even know I was in the room."

"Why always midnight to 8 a.m.?" another participant asked.

"Because that's when her vampires emerge in the alleys and streets, when she meets them somewhere in New Orleans, when they find their hosts, get nourished and tell their stories. It's the only time she can write these books."

Nearly 25 years have passed since Stan spoke at that conference. This remains the single greatest description of the Creative Dream in action that I have heard.

All great writers operate in the Creative Dream, along with great filmmakers, artists, playwrights, musicians and songwriters. It's a wonderful playground: Everything is fair game, relationships form between the strangest bedfellows among words and thoughts, and stories sometimes seem to write themselves. The conscious, subconscious and superconscious minds merge like a pyramid and bring all of your relevant life experience, intuition and inspiration into the process. The surprises and revealed jewels are often rich and abundant. In an essay, "Still Life With Muse," I wrote:

> The Creative Dream, or direct contact with the Muse, is such a beautiful experience, yet it scares us. Why? Why

> don't we eagerly sit down at the computer, type out a page or two to warm up, then immerse as easily as hopping into a swimming pool in August? Because what we are doing is entering into a different reality. It is not a linear, task- and time-oriented process like that we use to structure and manage our daily lives. It is not dependent on other people, food or our other normal staples for sustenance. The Creative Dream gathers nourishment from a much higher and deeper source. It is a near-complete transcendence of what we know to be time and space. While our creative spirits know this and practically plead with us to be allowed to play, our minds resist with everything in their power. Anyone who has written fiction, poetry or song lyrics, or painted on a regular basis, knows the power of this resistance. The conscious, egoic mind will do anything to avoid being put on hold while the Muse emerges and delivers the dialogue, plot, character interaction, conflicts and resolutions over and over again.

We've all experienced the freedom, experiences, fantasies and nightmares of thousands of dreams. Consider the dreams you wanted to last forever, those journeys so full of texture, color, adventure, passion, fantasy, twists and turns that you don't want to imagine life on the other side of sleep's veil. These dreams sweep you into their core, make you the center of attention, and command your fullest attention as they spin into two, three, four different locations, time settings, or changes in your persona before returning you to waking consciousness. In some cases, your perception of the waking world has been altered or shaken; how many times have you felt a little discombobulated after a particularly powerful dream? The same "rules" apply to the Creative Dream.

The *real* writing, those universal truths that connect with the readers' hearts and souls, assemble and take form here. Our job is to let the stories and characters flow through us; we can polish later. The material that arises from deep within us is, as Marty Balin admonishes, "the material that you keep."

A few characteristics of the Creative Dream to remember:

1) **"My entire world consists of the story I'm writing. Nothing else."** Become so focused, so immersed in your story, essay or article that *nothing* else matters when you're writing.

2) **The Creative Dream lies beyond the workaday or task-driven world.** Sit down and begin to write. Go where the story takes you.

3) **Your ability to work in the Creative Dream is directly proportional to your ability to trust yourself.** *Trust* is the most important word in writing, or any form of creativity.

4) **Resist intrusions of the busybody, rational mind.** The waking mind and its linear approach runs against the grain of creativity. Try not to fight this resistance, but to detour around it by writing whatever is on your mind, as quickly as you can—and keep going until it takes you deep into your story or article. Then just *write.*

5) **The Creative Dream is a directed daydream.** Daydream on paper. Imagine a character or story. Fantasize in your journal. Wonder aloud in dialogue. Make your writing sessions adventures in directed daydreaming.

6) **Relax and immerse.** The more relaxed our minds and bodies, the more successful and rewarding our sessions. Affirm that you're going to produce what you need from the day's session—then trust what happens next.

APPLY & INTEGRATE

Prolific writers operate with well-honed habits that enable them to slip into the Creative Dream every day and produce quality work. Part of growing as a writer is to refine our lives and work habits so that we can flow creatively on a regular basis. The more amenable we make our home and work environment, the greater our chances of enjoying long, enriching sessions. Consider:

- **Surrounding yourself with creative creature comforts.** Make sure your chair is comfortable and your area is properly lit. Perhaps learn to Feng Shui your office, as that will create the most fertile environment for creative work. In my "educated man's cave," as I like to call my office, I'm surrounded by books, music, plants, good track lighting, and bright-colored paintings. My computer is positioned so I can look out on the sky and trees through my window. The pictures on my wall include: an aerial shot of the shoreline of my hometown, Carlsbad, taken during my teen years; a couple of marathon race photos; a portrait of Mozart performing – with a sheet music backdrop – that I picked up in Salzburg; a great surfing poster signed by Clay Marzo, my subject in *Just Add Water*; sweeping prints of angels and goddesses, who I like to think drop into the Creative Dream to sprinkle a little ambrosia on our stories; and a photo of a Key West beach chair, painted in the oranges, blues and fiery oranges of a Conch Republic sky at sunrise. "License to Chill," it reads. In this environment, it's not hard immersing. That's the goal.
- **Writing while facing a window.** Look beyond your four walls into whatever world you're bringing onto the paper. Also, seek a view of nature or a verdant garden. This will stimulate your inner vision, the driving force of the Creative Dream.
- **Creating set times for writing each day**, especially if you are working on a book, short story, essay or a collection. If you're a parent or fully employed, flip a coin—early morning or late night. Both are optimal times for creativity (and likely your only options). Train your mind to be ready. When you sit down, make that the only activity for the next several hours. Get up to take stretching breaks every hour or so—if you are even cognizant of the time, not always the case! Inform other family members that you're not to be disturbed except for urgent matters. Turn off your phone. Stay offline.
- **Going deep, immediately.** Don't dabble in yesterday's work, except to review where you left off. Move forward and let the subject of your writing take over. Resist your mind's ceaseless attempts to control the action. Avoid

circling back to edit during this process. You will have plenty of time after the session.

- **Keeping a notebook to jot down ideas that spring up.** When you are in the Creative Dream, ideas will flow from all directions. Catch them with a quick note. Sometimes, these ideas will result in stories, poems, letters or articles. Sometimes, they are matters that will be addressed later in your book. By writing them down, your memory will be sparked. You won't lose any momentum with your work-in-progress.

When you are finished, allow yourself to "re-enter" the regular world. It sometimes really does feel like we're on a spacewalk or another otherworldly endeavor; in a sense, we are. I recommend a minimum of 30 minutes for every two hours spent in deep writing. Take a run or walk. Take a rejuvenating bath. Do a half-dozen yoga postures *slowly, deeply.* Go to the fitness center—if it's not crowded. Find a sweet spot in nature, sit, and decompress. Allow your body, mind and heart to assimilate the experience, and bring unfinished aspects of the story into your head for further percolation and development. Relax back into the phone calls, bills, kids, errands and meals that are waiting for you.

EXERCISES

- Write down a major event that took place in your life. Write 150 words about it. Now, underline the most poignant or striking sentence in your description. Depart from there, and write another 150 words. Repeat for two more rounds. See if you can feel the *essence* of the event more deeply, the impression it left behind in your intellectual and cellular memory. From that refined departure point, write for an hour. Allow the piece to "form itself," to turn and curve in whatever direction it takes. Follow with your pen or keystrokes. Forget about the busy world. When finished, see how the piece relates to the original event that started this exercise—and to each of the three sentences you underlined to get to this point.

- Begin every journal session with 5 to 10 minutes of brainstorming, or free writing.

- Whatever comes to mind first, run with it. Write as freely as a mustang galloping and rearing up on open range. Do not censor, edit nor encumber yourself. Spill your thoughts onto the page, flowing like a mountain spring.

- Take an existing journal entry, or a story or essay you've put aside, and write as if the ending does not matter. Let the story take you away. Let your imagination and folly run wild; write without any regard for the reader or your own preconceived notions.

- Create a character. It can be an aspect of yourself, a figment of your imagination, or a depiction of someone you passed on the street. Give that character a name, a face and a way of speaking. Dialogue back-and-forth. Write only dialogue. When the character starts to "speak" freely, don't stop what is being "said." Do this for 30 to 45 minutes.

- Metaphor Exercise: Metaphors are the rubies of the writer's crown. They are phrases, sentences or paragraphs that create instant connection, sometimes give deeper meaning to life, and are often quite memorable. Some of the best arise in the Creative Dream, which is why it is so important to learn how to craft them. Take one of the most famous metaphors in American literature, from Stephen Crane's *The Red Badge of Courage:* "The sun was a red wafer in the sky." He was writing about a Civil War battlefield. From this image, we feel ourselves on a field of blood (red), asking for God's intercession (red wafer – Catholic symbol of communion – lifting up to God), and imagining cannon and gunpowder smoke from the eeriness of the sentence. Crane painted that entire picture in eight words, which leads to the power of metaphor: it draws us immediately into a scene.

We can consciously construct metaphors to learn the skill, and then allow our superconscious minds to take over during writing sessions. The key is to pair solid concrete nouns with other nouns that reflect an aspect of the first noun, but seem to be unrelated on the surface.

First, write down 10 nouns you'd like to turn into metaphors. Now, write down 10 other nouns. Finally, write down 10 adjectives—particularly colors, and dynamic descriptive words (sharp, swift, deep, hot, solid, powerful, etc.). Mix and match in groups of three until you have something from which you can write a sentence. Write one sentence for each group.

To finish, take the sentence that sparks you the most. Write a solid paragraph from there, sticking tight to the metaphor, then drawing it out. See if you can unfurl the metaphor into a scene, a moment, something that reaches in and grabs you, gives you a different perspective on your subject noun. When finished, either go further with this paragraph, or take another sentence and write.

Q&A TAKEAWAY

Q: What are the advantages of immersing into the Creative Dream, rather than logically moving from one outlined paragraph to the next?

A: We need (and should employ) outlines to serve as narrative roadmaps for our work, no matter whether we're writing newsletter pieces, articles, or books. However, we also need our inner world if we're to write creatively *and* touch our readers. By immersing into the Creative Dream, we connect with the same invisible source as that which brings life itself into being. Stories flow (apparently) effortlessly, insights pop up we never considered, and we live through what we write. Our writing becomes part of us, rather than apart from us.

Q: At what point do I "let go" of what I had planned to write and allow my creative mind to "guide" the story?

A: When your writing starts flowing and sentences move smoothly, and your subject seems to be "spilling onto the page," then ride the creative wave and see what happens. Likely, you will find yourself looking at very strong material, often material that solves problems you'd been having with the story. Your creative mind is now in charge—and you have already engrained your plan subconsciously. At this point, let it fly!

Q: What are some of the ways in which I can develop and nurture my creative mind?

A: Talk to strange, eccentric, creative people living their lives in unique ways. Visit museums, galleries, and library exhibits. Attend concerts in a genre outside your comfort zone. Play trance, classical, or atmosphere music while writing. Try magnetic poetry. Take up a creative hobby, such as drawing, painting, sculpting, or landscape gardening. Look for other creative channels, knowing they all will funnel back and feed your writing somehow.

Q: Does it work to write whatever comes to me if I am simultaneously working on another project? Or should I jot down the idea and wait until I'm done?

A: Yes. And Yes. If you're working on a project, and an idea races through your mind like a fugitive comet being pursued, switch gears and *get that idea down!* You do not know with certainty it will circle back for a return visit. Write what you can, making sure to capture how the idea *feels* to you, then return to your project. Later, when you have time, get into your journal and flesh out the idea.

FOUR

Practice Presence

The point of power is in the present. Turn your writing into an active, vibrant celebration of the present moment.

"Within every sentence lies the seed to write the entirety of our life experience."

—Robert Yehling

Reknowned naturalist Joseph Cornell once told students on the Navajo Indian Reservation: "Draw a picture of yourself." The author of *Sharing the Joy of Nature* expected to receive a colorful stack of stick figures, exaggerated expressions, and other caricatures and depictions that showed how the child viewed himself or herself.

Something else happened. One portrait ably represented a number of surprises Cornell received from his audience: The student was a small figure in the middle of a drawing of canyons, cornfields, fluffy cotton clouds, a bolt of lightning and family members. The only colors he used in the drawing were red, brown, sand, black, and blue—the primary colors of the Northeastern Arizona-Northwestern New Mexico landscape, where the Navajo Reservation is located. His self-portrait showed complete connection with his surrounding environment. In the boy's view, the high Arizona desert was as much a part of him as his nose and mouth.

When Cornell first told me this story, shivers ran up and down my spine. It spoke of the reverence Native Americans hold toward nature; they see no separation from themselves. They derive their spirituality, cosmology, medicine, sustenance, lodging and relationship with life from nature; the natural world *is* their life, individually and collectively. Landscape, present awareness, and connection to Great Spirit create for them what Gary Snyder calls "a place in space." The students made that very clear in the drawings they delivered to Cornell. When I shared this story with eminent Native American author/poet/musician Joy Harjo, whose *Brave Warrior* is one of the best memoir/poetry works in print, she wrote back, "For us, there is not just this world, there's also a layering of others. Everything has presence and meaning within this landscape of timelessness."

If trust is the most important behavioral quality for a writer—along with discipline—then presence is the central state of being. The point of power is in the present. The past is over; we can't change it. The future hasn't happened yet; why worry or project any more than necessary? We're left with the here and now, the junction of our past experiences (and lessons learned), future aspirations, and all that we are and know today. It's an incredibly powerful place, where everything happens—especially if we're focused on the moment. Attention, concentration, creativity and potential join at this point. Only through presence can we enter the Creative Dream. Only through presence can we truly observe and perceive something, connect with our intuition to gain insight, take our next steps forward . . . and write something fresh and new.

The little Navajo boy encompassed everything that fed him, but he put himself in the center, in the place where his entire Circle of Life comes together. A yoga aphorism, derived from the words of Indian poet Rabindranath Tagore, says: "Center everywhere, circumference nowhere." Eckhart Tolle refers to it as "the power of NOW." When we're operating in a state of presence, we feel like we're a part of everything that concerns or interests us—and those things are a part of us. We see life at this moment in all its 360 degrees, as our most distant ancestors did in order to know their environment and the dangers it presented. Every moment is a miniature Circle of Life. If this state reminds you vaguely of something, it might be yourself in your earliest years, prior to entering the school system and learning how to navigate rules and structured schedules. Some can handle it, and others have trouble. All healthy people possess the 360-degree mind, "the hunter's mind" as author Thom Hartmann calls it. Presence is not a matter of worrying about tomorrow's errands or yesterday's parent-teacher conference, nor is it daydreaming about your weekend plans or the incredible nature hike you took last month. When you write, direct your focus on your story as it rolls through your fingertips *right now*. If you can do this, we will feel the presence in everything you write, as if we are experiencing your story, thoughts, perceptions or feelings right now.

A quick exercise: For the next 3-5 minutes, write down everything you are thinking, feeling, observing, or desiring. Don't lift your pen up, and don't correct a sentence or even change a word. Just write. When you're finished, read your piece and look for its state of presence. Are your verbs in present tense? Are you writing about the here-and-now, the been-and-gone, or the not-here-yet?

Presence animates your story and keeps readers fully engaged. Everything falls within the presence *of the story*, its timeline, the "eternal now," if you will. Characters are in the moment, whether dressed in togas or spacesuits. Everything they say is relevant to *their* time. We walk in their footsteps, whether we're picking heather and thyme with our fellow villagers in a medieval English countryside, dealing with building a new life from the rubble of the old in a poignant memoir, or exploring the backside of Mars. Not only does the narrative feel present, but all good dialogue is written as though you are standing in the middle of the conversation.

The tactical key to writing from a state of presence lies with *action verbs*. They make everything we write active and present, alive and vibrant, focused and engaged, which makes sense: don't we feel the same when we take actions? Consider the difference between these two sentences:

"I was walking down the street."
and
"I strolled along the tree-lined street, whistled with the birds, and watched two lovers frolic on the hillside."

One sentence is a freeze-dried meal; the other, by comparison, feels like a small senory feast that pulls you into the moment. The difference? The first sentence doesn't give any hint as to the emotional state of the subject. The second sentence not only shows light-heartedness ("strolled," "whistled"), but use of the verb "strolled," rather than "was walking," opens up the moment to be fully described. Even written in past tense, we can easily imagine ourselves joining the lucky person who experienced this moment.

Another key to writing in a state of presence involves history, background, and vernacular. If you're writing a letter, you will share the latest news, and write it in your voice, whether the way you speak or a more refined writing style. If you're writing a story set in the 18th century, however, you will need to work with vernacular and cultural references pertaining to that era. The difference is stark: If I see a mobile phone mentioned in a story about the American Revolution, I won't be reading any further. Likewise, if we're sitting on a Hawaiian beach with your character, a very local islander, we will not expect to hear slang and dialect out of the South. However, if your character talks in Hawaiian Pidgin dialect and speaks to elements like the ocean, mountains, fish and waves, then we have no trouble slipping into the world you created.

Of the historical novels I've edited, one of the best at driving home the power of presence is *My Interview With Beethoven,* by L.S. Jones, scheduled to be released in late 2016. In the story, a young turn-of-the-19th century Virginia newspaperman believes he is the illegitimate child of Beethoven, so he sails to Europe and interview the great deaf maestro. It's extremely difficult to carry an interview in fiction writing for 50 pages, let alone 400, but Jones delivers with excruciating attention to the details that make a historical novel sing, everything in its proper place. And *time.* An example:

> How did I lose Rathburn's favor? I'll tell y'all: I was born into a tangled nest of lies. Lies flow in my blood. Small wonder I chose the press, the most profane and vilified of professions. The press permits me to twist truths, weave tales, and toy with people's heads. The press also permits me easy access to Northern newspapers, which gladly published my articles against slavery, the South's "peculiar institution." Naturally, I hid my correspondences from Rathburn and any other Southerner. Had they been found, my compositions would have served my undoing. More than my effigy would have hung from a tree.

All of this convinced me that a nobler path existed with Beethoven, whose music leaves nothing unsaid or unturned. He awes me still, excites my imagination, soothes my troubled demons, and emboldens me with nerve. I want to sail to meet him. I will like him once I meet him. He will embrace me as good fathers do, and shake off the rocks and briars from the paths I set for myself. "My interview with Beethoven will happen," I convinced myself, "and finally my life will be fine—even if I have to lie to make that happen."

A quick breakdown of these two paragraphs shows the power of presence in several ways:

1) The author uses present-tense action verbs throughout. She sets it as if 1805 is happening right now.

2) She alludes to North vs. South, very much a hot-button issue in the early 19th century.

3) She uses descriptives from a different time: "compositions"; "shake off the rocks and briars"; "I want to sail."

4) The very fact she writes about Beethoven in present time sets the moment.

And yet, the author also reaches beyond her chosen time period, connecting to a larger presence, the universal (and slightly less than universal) truths that pertain to any time, because they are *life truths* expressed within George Thompson, the interviewer: "lies flow in my blood"; "he awes me still, excites my imagination, soothes my troubled demons, and emboldens me with nerve"; or "he will embrace me as good fathers do." And, I'm sure some will agree with George's opinion about the newspaper journalism profession; it sounds like it could be said today.

There are many ways to develop the still, ever-present mind that can perceive and observe everything. Quiet contemplation and solitude are great. Try silent forays into nature, using your time to deeply observe everything around you. I provide a nice writing exercise for this called "Zoom In, Zoom Out" (see below). Meditation and prayer are ageless liberators of restless minds, as well as conduits between our outer worlds and inner selves. Even five minutes of receptive prayer or meditation can engage the Siamese twin of presence—the heart. It helps to curtail the cerebral chatterbox. Yoga, long walks and exercise alleviate tension and stress, which quiets body and mind. Take long, quiet walks before or after you write. Cut back on mindless TV viewing; if you need a fix, pop in a DVD or stream a well-written movie or documentary. Play quiet, uplifting music. *Slow* your pace, look more deeply into your immediate environment, and see if you feel like your heart and mind are both expanding, growing in the moment.

That is a healthy state of presence.

One of my favorite stories comes from a then-unknown actor in 1975. After knocking around on limited acting ability, Sylvester Stallone hit upon an idea. Over the next three days, his pen spilled story onto page. He worked through the scenario playing within his mind, never losing focus. When he was finished, he stared down at the raw *Rocky* screenplay, soon the nexus of a multi billion-dollar franchise that encompassed four movies, took a generation's respite, then returned with 2015's acclaimed *Creed.* His presence (and, no doubt, his growling stomach) vaulted him to superstardom. Handel composed *The Messiah* in a similar way, only under even more extreme conditions. When a kernel of the eventual masterpiece dropped into his imagination, Handel felt his soul ignite. That was all the push he needed: for the next 72 hours, he worked non-stop, blazing like a firestorm, writing down the notes as quickly as the music poured through him. He turned away all visitors and food; he never left his small room. He stayed in the presence of the work. We have rejoiced in the outcome for the past two centuries.

Literature abounds with such tales of ferocious creativity. Beat novelist Jack Kerouac, wrote in short, intense bursts that, to any writer, feel like land speed records: Three days to write *The Subterraneans.* Twelve days to write *The Dharma Bums,* considered his second masterpiece behind On The Road. One of his sentences in *The Subterraneans* is *1,200 words.* When I read it aloud to one of my college students, with whom I'd crafted a semester-long course in Beat writing, his jaw dropped. So did mine, from exhaustion after reading for 10 minutes straight. And yet, this sentence *moved.* It *grooved.* It twisted, turned, rose, fell, and socked you right in the heart. It did exactly as Kerouac intended, capturing the feeling of a jazz man blowing his horn in a smoky, dark subterranean club (hence, the title).

Presence is our birthright as writers and human beings. Stay present and mindful, send your past and future concerns where they belong, and you will soon find your own miracles spilling onto the page—over and over again. After all, you can only write of the past or future; you cannot write within them.

APPLY & INTEGRATE

The ability to write in presence or "the eternal now"—the place of the heart, soul, and our visionary mind—is of paramount importance. Our goal is to develop the capacity to live in the present moment, so that when we write, we can bring forth fullest awareness of our subject matter. Some ideas and tips on how to proceed:

- Before starting the new day with your work-in-progress, close your eyes and take a few moments to get present and centered. When disparate thoughts arise (and they will; the ego will constantly battle the superconscious, creative state for control of your next thought), just say, "I'll get back to you later." When your mind truly feels clear, then open your eyes and write.
- Visualize your story or essay playing on a movie screen. Everything is blacked out around you. It's just you and the movie screen. Write the images, characters, situations and resolutions as they manifest and develop on the screen.
- Step up your practice of silent contemplation, prayer, sitting meditation, or walking meditation—whatever facilitates your inner peace and calmness and sharpens your outer focus. Most prolific writers are contemplative masters of maintaining long periods of silence and solitude. Take this step, and increase your practice every week.
- When editing your work, eliminate most passive ("to be") verbs – was, were, are, have, had, going, etc. Sometimes they're necessary, but in most cases, they reflect the writer's "armchair traveler" position in the story. Also, they create lazy writing. Live in the center of the story, in its full presence. Use action verbs whenever possible.

EXERCISES

- Power Words: Write out 20 to 25 verbs, nouns and colors that resonate within you—that give you a little "spark." For instance, five of my words are "angel," "stride," "fire," "ocean" and "green." Buy a packet of index cards and put one word on each card. Then shuffle the deck and pull seven words. Arrange them in an order that makes some sense, and write 250 to 1,000 words from that beginning.

- From the power words, select five nouns or verbs that evoke a particular feeling of strength, power, happiness or joy within you. All should denote action or something visible and powerful. Write sentences or paragraphs using these words. *Feel* how they activate you creatively.

- Write a 500- to 1,000-word piece, a letter, or a poem starting NOW. Use action verbs to move your subjects around. Describe what you see, and how you feel/think about it. Describe your setting as though it were alive, vibrant. Show how you are centrally positioned in this moment.

- For dreamers: The next time you remember a dream, write it out as though it were happening in your conscious life. How would it change your life? How would the dream evolve? Stay in the present tense with your verbs.

- For non-fiction writers: Take a headline from the newspaper or a candid moment from your life. Plant yourself in that setting as it looks right here, right now. What do you see? What do you feel? What are your surroundings? How are you a part of the moment? How are you moving? What are you touching? How does the moment attract or repel you?

- Select a dynamic time period that fascinates you with its history, society, culture, or adventurism. Anytime in history will do. Imagine yourself dropped into the time. Describe in one page what surrounds you, how you feel, and any events taking place. Use only present-tense, action verbs. Make it feel like this time period is occuring today.

Q&A TAKEAWAY

Q: How do I assimilate reading, research and life experience, and then construct it as as present-moment writing?

A: Just write! Focus on everything you can bring to the subject, and let it fly on the page. I often use the Comment bar on my Word program to jot notes to self while writing, to remind myself to verify a fact, detail, story or finding—a product of my reading and research. Or, a story of something that happened five years ago that is germaine to the text might pop up. Off to the Comment bar I go. It's a great tool.

Q: How can I better write with action verbs to drive my stories and create constant presence?

A: By practicing with action verbs. After writing a passage, go back and find the passive, "to be" verbs (was going, were walking, had been, etc.). See if you can replace them with action verbs—traveled, strolled, etc. Take a step further, and increase your action verb dexterity. All good novels and creative non-fiction teem with them; authors know how to drive narrative. Study sports pages and sports articles; this writing thrives on verbs. If you write an ordinary action verb, such as "walk," see if you can replace it with a synonym that better reflects the actual movement of the subject: stroll, amble, stumble, cruise, hike, etc. Each depicts a specific type of movement and action. You *show* the movement with the verb, rather than *describing or telling* it with added words. That's the goal. Action verbs reflect direct, present life experience.

Q: In what areas of my writing do I slow down or "hold back" from what I'm really trying to say?

A: I still struggle with this occasionally, after 40 years! Our minds are mighty machines that race past our ability to write everything down. Focus on how your subject makes/made you feel, how it affected you, and what happened next. If you can include these three elements into a piece of writing, you'll climb right into what you want to say. Also, try to avoid phrases like "I remember," "Way back when," "Long ago," etc. Those knock the reader off track, because the reader suspends his/her daily life to enter another experience—the experience you present in words. You're left with *presence,* through words, saying what needs to be said in that moment.

FIVE

Perpetual Adventure of Discovery

When we regard every life experience as an adventure that leads to a discovery, big or small, we touch the core of all good writing: the process of journey and discovery.

"Discovery consists of looking at the same thing as everyone else and thinking something different."

—Albert Szent-Györgi, Nobel Prize–winning physiologist

During a workshop at Munich's Gasthaus Rosengarten, a major snowfall turned the Bavarian landscape into a winter wonderland. As I trudged through knee-deep snow toward the conference room's back entrance before beginning the second day of the workshop, I already sensed magic in the air.

So did the workshop participants, already buzzing from their morning *schwarzentee* fix and the fresh, dry powder outside, thoughts of having to shovel their driveways temporarily blocked like a boulder-covered road. Rosengarten's namesake, the twenty-acre rose garden, was covered in a soft white cloak rimmed by pines, firs and cedars. An elderly Bavarian couple passed through the garden in traditional dress—hats, heavy coats, scarves, as if materializing from another era. What stopped my breath was how they traversed the snowscaped garden: in a horse-drawn sleigh . . .

I mentally transported two centuries back, when music, literature and conversation reigned in salons and cafes among a cathedral of forests, villages with red-roofed taverns and churches, and cobbled alleys and streets diving in all directions, medieval cities and castles wrapped in Bavaria's charm. I lingered in my reverie until the group finished writing, imagining Germany's greatest creative genius, Johann Wolfgang von Goethe, wove together nature, linguistics, travel, passion and discovery into his voluminous works—enough to fill nearly 150 books, each 500 pages.

Infused with present awareness, genetic memory and a strong sense of adventure, I was ready to set sail with my pen. Likewise, the 30 participants were supercharged the entire day. Each discovered something new about themselves through their words and the transformed landscape. All while sitting in a toasty inn, robust flames licking the hearth, a scene that embodied the famous lyric "chestnuts roasting on an open fire." Which they'd been doing in street markets all winter. Wrote one participant later, "I never really understood how writing not only opens you up to discovery, but is discovery . . . and creates the spirit of discovery."

Good writing boils down to four things: Presence. Storytelling. Clear communication. And discovery. Discovery and its life experience soulmate, adventure, walk hand-in-hand, tethered by presence, awareness, and mindfulness. One feeds the other; both are vital for successful writing (and purposeful living.) Think of reaching the trailhead of a hike, looking at the sign and distance options, and choosing a path. Sometimes, we race along, focused on our destination, chatting with fellow hikers, spirits rising upon the sweep of the majestic day. However, the deeper adventure comes from concentrating on every step, absorbing every sight or perception along the way, all 12 senses engaged, our consciousness sharp and heightened as a golden eagle on the hunt. Every sentence fills with the power and energy of its predecessor nouns, verbs and adjectives. Every sentence moves the adventure along while adding discovery—of a geologic formation, animal or bird, how the wind touches the skin, an inner feeling that surfaces. Some sentences are sparse, others plump and pregnant as the expectant mother of triplets.

The hike continues, one step and sentence at a time, the windy, rocky, undulating path adding to both its beauty and challenge. Your consciousness, senses, and pen synch up, driving you more inward, into the deeper adventure, discovering more and more nuances about subject and self with every movement. Once the trail ends, you learn, feel, perceive or conclude something new. The discovery. Looking over your shoulder, you see a trail of footprints, completed steps—and, if writing, the dozens or hundreds of sentences, each an adventure unto itself, that led to this point.

The beauty of this approach? It works wonders, no matter whether you are hiking in the Alps or writing a story about how you came upon your latest recipe. After all, what is more engaging? A recipe on an index card? Or the story of how the ingredients, ideas and adventure of making the dish resulted in the recipe? With that question comes the secret of why story-driven recipe books always sell like hotcakes: because you're not just reading a recipe. You're going on the *adventure* that creates the dish.

Which leads to one of my favorite examples. In the Fall of 2012, I received a call from Tim Martin, for whom I'd edited two novels. He was calling on behalf of his wife, Lynne, who'd just picked up a *Wall Street Journal* assignment about their lifestyle. What a lifestyle it was: Lynne, a retired L.A. boutique PR agency owner, and Tim, who once wrote songs for classic rock bands like Blood, Sweat & Tears, put a fresh spin on retirement. They turned into elder gypsies. While staring at the clock in their California home, the Martins looked at each other and said, "What in the hell are we doing? Let's get out of here and live in the world." In the next year, they sold their home and downsized a lifetime of possessions until the remainder fit into a 10 x 20 storage shed. Tim also spent time on the computer, booking reservations and budgeting costs, until he realized something: Living abroad would be cheaper than staying home!

When the Martins called me, they had already spent two years in flats, castles, inns, houses, ships, penziones, *guest houses,* guests of houses, and plenty of other domiciles in Buenos Aires, San Miguel de Allende, Florence, Istanbul, Marrakech, London, and their favorite, Paris. Among others. They rarely stayed in one place for more than three months. They started a blog, homefree-adventures.com, chronicling their living adventure and offering pointers for others thinking of living elsewhere.

All the elements were in place for a great book—only Lynne did not know how to write one. She was a print journalist and publicist by trade. With the momentum of the *Wall Street Journal* piece (which got more online readers in the third week of October, 2012, than the coverage of presidential candidates Barack Obama and Mitt Romney combined), I approached my agent, who took on Lynne and sold the book. It became a *New York Times* and Amazon.com bestseller upon its release in April 2014, and Lynne found herself a regular presenter at AARP conventions.

Now, Lynne had to write the book. For the next six months, we worked via Skype, email and text message. I "visited" with her in her living room in Portugal, in her Paris flat, and while she and Tim were renting a room in a stately manor outside Dublin. If

I ever write a book about adventures in editing, this is exhibit No. 1! In coaching, guiding, and editing Lynne's materials, I kept her focused on these points, which are the heart and soul of writing adventure and discovery:

- Every sentence leads to the next.
- Write the experience—then describe what you perceived, how you feel, what you took in. (Remember, we can carry everything we see into our inner world.)
- Focus on sights, sounds, tastes, scents, styles, figures of speech and ways of doing things we don't see in the U.S.—but which help define the place.
- Use action verbs, words that *move* the sentences. You can capture the entire feeling and impact of a scene by showing the action and using strong verbs. Show, don't tell.
- State the outcome. What did you take out of the experience that helps you in future.
- Everything moves. Everything is a movement. Even standing still and being silent.

If presence is the beacon of writing, then adventure and discovery make up its beating heart. It is the pulse, the driving force of finding, learning or realizing something, that makes the next moment appear *new* in its most original, primal sense. It is the natural rhythm of our life: we have been hard-wired to explore and discover for all 100,000 years (thereabouts) of *homo sapiens'* presence on earth; it's right there, in our brain stem, our most primal instinct. Our distant Paleolithic predecessors explored, adventured, and discovered for food and shelter; we have greater luxury to use these instincts. It doesn't matter whether you're writing a letter, travelogue, poetry, autobiography, fiction, picture captions, clothing hangtag blurbs or business proposals. If ever we were to inject slices of our lives into our writing, this is where it happens—by turning our writing into a feeling of adventure and discovery, no matter the subject. That is why memoir has been so popular the past thirty years: we get caught up in another's life story, their process of self-*discovery,* and the experiences and processes (adventure) of getting there. *Simply put, writing in the spirit of adventure and discovery moves your work forward and keeps the reader engaged.*

One of my favorite film stories concerns the brilliant German director, Leni Riefenstahl, and how she used discovery in all its facets when making *The Blue Light* (1931). It is the story of a young woman's quest to keep intact her discovery of a blue light in a hilly Italian grotto while fighting off villagers and established artists who want to destroy the light. To the girl, the light represents her greatest self-expression, her highest idealism. The film's plot is a stirring study of self-discovery. "In making this very romantic film by instinct, *without knowing exactly where I wanted to go* (my emphasis), I also found myself expressing the path that would be mine later," said Riefenstahl.

Likewise, when I worked with Marty Balin on his memoir, *Full Flight: Adventures with Airplanes and Starships,* you know which chapter received the highest compliments? The Chapter in which I recounted our walk down San Francisco's Haight Street on a June day in 2000, where Jefferson Starship's re-fabricated lineup was performing. Marty was one of the five or six central scenemakers on Haight Street from 1965 through the Summer of Love, so plenty of people came up to show their love. Meanwhile, I'd just written a cover story on Marty for a national magazine—which was window merchandised in a few of the shops as we walked by. Midway through thre show, Marty grabbed a temporary roadie's open cellphone, walk to center stage, and sing into the phone and mic. Besides the 50,000 people on the street, Marty was serenading the roadie's wife; they'd become engaged while listening to Marty's epic hit "Miracles" on the radio in the mid-70s, and the roadie wanted her to hear it from the show. It's just that he (nor she) expected the personal serenade. I've covered rock and pop music for 35 years. This remains *the* nicest thing I've seen a performer do live. All part of the adventure.

As a huge Jefferson Airplane fan, and a fan of the consciousness, music and spirit-lifting aspects of the '60s, I was on a cloud. I turned that chapter into a single-movement adventure, my eyes open on behalf of readers. I also reprised and fictionalized parts of it in my novel, *Voices.*

Why did this chapter resonate so strongly? Because readers felt they took the half-mile walk with us. They joined our adventure, and we gave them quite the tour—capped by Marty's openhearted gesture. No surprise, since in the '60s, he was known in

San Francisco's psychedelic rock scene as "the man you go to when you want to write a love ballad."

Think of four or five of the greatest discovery or adventure books you've read, whether an inner or outer adventure/discovery. Write down the titles of your chosen books, and in three or four sentences, describe the way in which each story moved you. What feelings did the book evoke? Into which places did it plant you? How was the sense of adventure, mystery, intrigue or exploration conveyed—and why did it resonate so deeply for you?

When I travel to Venice, or sit at the ruins of the love-scorned Roman poet Catullus' villa on the nearby peninsula of Sirmione, I feel Goethe's presence and his words everywhere; his descriptions expand my discovery of two of his favorite Italian haunts. Watch how Goethe tied together discovery and writing, leaving no room for separation: "Such was the beginning of that course from which I have been unable throughout my life to deviate: I mean the conversion of whatever delighted, distressed or otherwise preoccupied me into an image, a poem, thus finishing with it; so as both to rectify my notions of exterior things, and to tranquilize myself within."

Write like an explorer discovering new lands. With your next journal entry, letter, poem, essay or story, become infused with the magic, innocence and wisdom of your subject—the sense of wonder—*before* writing. Fill with wonder—wonder-fill, *wonderful*—completely as you hitch up your rucksack of research, characters, outlines and life experience, and hike with your own words. If a strange path of images, dialogue or another angle of your topic appears, take it. The worst thing that can happen is that you need to return to the main path after expanding yourself and your experience further by having risked that side trail. Write as if you're on an adventure, and we're coming along with you.

Give yourself permission to be wild and magnificent. It is innate in us, which is why we long to dance, explore, hike, swim in open oceans or play with our kids. We are filled with a longing for the wild; some of us have just suppressed it more than others. In our ordered world, we tend to view wildness as the distant province of antisocial behavior rather than an act of complete, full body-mind-soul expression. The Muse is a wild, expressive dancer. Nature is wild, beautiful and magnificent. So are we—if we give ourselves a chance. Release the inner censors and limitations placed by others and yourself—and writewith abandon. "Wildness is the state of complete awareness," poet Gary Snyder says. "That's why we need it."

APPLY & INTEGRATE

Return to the scenes of your greatest trips and journeys. If necessary, use travel journals, photographs, recent magazine features or books about the place or articles you wrote at the time to stimulate your memory. Recall the feelings of discovery, magic, wonder and adventure, the almost overloaded sensory stimulation, the noises, smells, landscapes and faces. Remember that remarkable feeling of absolute presence? That is the bull's eye to hit every day when you write. Make your goal for *every* writing session to wind through your subject like Joseph Conrad in *The Heart of Darkness,* not knowing what lurks around the corner. Yet, you are so filled with the thrill of discovery and adventure that your readers cannot help but ride along in open-mouthed wonder—turning page after page. Even if your adventure is as "ordinary" as cleaning your room—and finding your Dad's old albums in a closet corner. Or, discovering that your somewhat rebellious teen is looking at old fashion magazines you've had around for 25 years, learning about you in another way.

EXERCISES

- For fiction writers: Create a destination story: one character, one journey, one day. Why is the character there? What is he/she trying to resolve? How will the setting of your story contribute to this resolution? Pick a place to which you have traveled. Write a 500- to 2,000 word short-story that focuses on the pure discovery the character feels (drawn, in whole or in part, from your sense of discovery when you were there).
- For non-fiction writers: Go back to the most adventurous or outrageous experience of your life—or one of the greatest self-discoveries you made. Recapture the feeling and replay some of the moments in your mind. Move back to

present while holding the *feeling.* Write a 500- to 1,000-word vignette or essay in which a typical day becomes a liberating romp. Cut loose; be wild and magnificent. Feel the presence and the power. Feel the soul call of the writer-as-artist.

- Adventure Triplets: Walk outside with a journal to a place that grabs your eye. Sit, focus deeply on that object or area, and write about it as though you see it for the first time. What do you see? If an object, what is it telling you about its story? Write in a three-sentence pattern. In your first sentence, write the action or observation. Next, what do you discover from it? Finally, how do you feel, or how does it change the way you're looking at the object or spot? Then repeat. Try to write for three rounds.
- Recall the most adventurous journey of your life. Turn to a menial task before you and write about it *while still feeling your adventurous journey.*
- If I said to you right now, "Cut loose—be completely wild for the next ten minutes," what would you do? Where would you go? Who would be your accomplice in wildness? Write with complete abandon for 10 minutes, then 20, then an hour. Keep going. Let go and embrace your wild side.

Q&A TAKEAWAY

Q: When I discover something new about a place, a person, an event or myself, how do I put those feelings and sensations into written form?

A: Think like a business opportunist. Stop what you're doing, and write what you're feeling *this second.* Use action verbs and concrete nouns. Write the experience; don't think twice about the words that spill out. Make this a habit.

Q: How do I develop journal writing into perpetual travelogue, where every entry becomes a trek of discovery and adventure? How do I then transfer this to my other writing?

A: By simply finding the sense of adventure in everything you do or think about, and writing the adventure. Show your feelings as you write. Connect them to the activity or adventure. Locate the thrills, chills, highs, lows, best sightings and *best insights.* Take one step at a time, one sentence at a time, like rock climbing.

Q: What are some ways to experience the magic, innocence and wonder that constantly surrounds my life?

A: This depends on your favorite activities, but a sure way is to take a walk in a natural setting, or a place of spectacular sights and architecture, shut off your busybody mind, and absorb what you see. Imagine how an eight-year-old would regard the moment. Consider how it was created, the countless right actions, steps or decisions that led up to it. Marvel at its sheer beauty or presence, without labeling or forming an opinion. Simply soak in the remarkable combination of factors that created that building. Or forest. Or blade of grass.

SIX

Microscopes & Telescopes

Ralph Waldo Emerson said, "The core of nature is in the heart of every man." Use inner and outer observation to deepen, animate, and enrich the simplest moments—or the most complex topics.

"If a writer stops observing, he is finished."

—Ernest Hemingway

We scattered like seeds into the southeastern New Mexico morning. For thirty minutes, we retreatants sat near a chattering creek and observed sky, earth, trees, birds, stream smells, and scents as they interacted with the wind, what author John Fox calls "the poetry of the earth." Each person roamed an area no larger than 20 by 20 feet. The goal was to observe everything in a small space, immerse in the present moment, and feel. *Then write. We stretched our inner and outer senses and focused on the not-so-obvious, such as:*

- What messages does the wind carry from a bird? A tree? The sky?
- What or who *used* to be here? What is their story?
- What music do I hear in the ground? The wind? My heart?
- How do these smells, winds and bird songs *taste*?
- What are the dominant and subtle landscape features? Why do they fit here?

We wrote quickly, trying to reel in what we observed and flow with the words that followed, rather than letting our minds define or compartmentalize. We wrote as though we were witnessing the majesty and the subtleties of dawn's creation in this place—which, in a sense, we were.

You didn't have to ask me twice. I became a sweet-toothed child running loose inside a Swiss chocolatier's warehouse! I rattled off ten stanzas, later to become a poetic suite called "Riverstone Runes." I sensed the invisible presence of a restless young man who, more than a century before, sat amongst these cottonwoods, oaks and poplars for a rare moment of respite—Billy the Kid. The Hondo Valley was his primary hideaway. Like William Bonney's likely state of mind while being pursued, jumpy and observant, the first two stanzas poured through on awareness and adrenalin:

They say William Bonney rode
Along this creek
After gunning down Tunstall
Sat on this embankment
Fed his horse
Hid from the Feds
As the cottonwoods
Fluttered from a constant wind,
Bonney's brother flight-spirit
Whispered to the creek: Hear the legend?

A decade and a thousand miles away, I sat in the Animim Forest on the Sierra Nevada's San Juan Ridge, recalling this experience with a dozen college students. I reprised the exercise that led to "Riverstone Runes," with a few variations. I asked them to focus their entire concentration and awareness on a five-foot circle around and above themselves—and write what they saw. Then, I asked them to extend the circle to 10 feet, and do the same. Then 25 feet, 50 feet, and finally, 100 feet out. What do you see? How do the elements, creatures and your mind and heart interact? What additional observations do you bring in with the longer view? How does the world around you expand?

After they finished, I gave them the news: we were only halfway through the exercise. I expected moans and groans, but instead, I noticed something else: my students were immersed in their setting, in their writing. So we reversed course, pulling their lens of observation inward . . . from 100 feet to 50 . . . 50 to 25 . . . 25 to 10 to five feet. Impressively, but not surprisingly, their "inbound" observations contained more subtleties in the world of that circle, a sense of deeper interaction. Their "outbound" writing was like viewing the world through a telescope, taking in all the sights and sounds. Then they brought it in, their inner and outer eyes capturing nuances, like a microscope. "It's like zooming in and zooming out with a camera lens," one student said.

Later, we reprised this exercise and trained it on different projects, from writing about relationship to creating sci-fi, fantasy, or other fictional settings. We used it for dialogue writing, journaling, and writing short-short stories. Whenever I or the students felt the need to throw off a creative shackle or two, we trotted out "Zoom In, Zoom Out," named from the comment made earlier. It has since become the favorite exercise I give at workshops, classrooms and conferences, as well as my "go-to" when I'm helping book clients and marketing communications writers break out of static or blind spots in their work and reach for wider vistas—and then bring them in, detail by detail.

Observation and its inner twin, perception, underpin writing. If you have trouble observing finer details, nuances of expression, or turns of mood or atmosphere, you will find it challenging to grab the reader's attention. We see through your eyes, hear through your ears, feel through the descriptions you give. How much can you observe in a single minute? Or second? What can you do with it? And, most importantly, how does it shape your world this moment? Or flow through you? When I think of these questions, I'm reminded of a remark from energy medicine expert Dr. Candace Pert—one I committed to memory: "Every second, a massive information exchange is occurring in your body. Imagine each of these messenger systems possessing a specific tone, humming a signature tune, rising and falling, waxing and waning, binding and unbinding."

What if we switched "story" with "massive information exchange?" Isn't an information exchange a story of sorts? Now look at that comment: there are a lot of potentially great stories within this miracle of ourselves. Enough to fill volumes. Within and behind Dr. Pert's words lie the deeper driving force of great memoirs, essays, stories, poems, songs . . . every form of subjective writing. If you connect with your reader at *this* level, and the reader feels your words deeply, then I want some of your magic potion. You've also got a fan for life. Simple as that.

Quick question: What color is the bark of the trees nearest you? If you say, "Green," or "Brown," or "White," one of my writing mentors, Pulitzer Prize-nominated poet/fictionist Harvey Stanbrough, will send you back into the grove or woods for a closer look. The primary color of an object is a first sighting, the telescopic look; the shades, hues, and patterns that feed it are the deeper observation, the microscope. One day, I took up Harvey's challenge while hiking in the White Mountains of New Hampshire. A river birch tree shed its bark in layers of brown, tan, gray, bird-dropping white, soft fluffy cloud, speckles of white and brown, each a different texture as well as color. When I looked again after a summer shower, I saw more than mushrooms sprouting. I watched a kaleidoscopic explosion of purples, yellows, greens, oranges, browns, tans and whites, shapes like cones, flying saucers, stovepipes, lampshades, a hen's tailfeathers. They had names like Hen of the Woods, Wood's Ear, Chantrelle, Morel.

A decade later, while hiking in the Austrian Alps near Salzburg, my eyes and senses zoomed into the hillsides and found decayed logs, mushrooms (same as those in New Hampshire, amazingly!), moss, lichens, insects, and two dozen shades of brown and green. I observed (zoom out), perceived (zoom in), and then committed to body memory—and my journal. Ten years from now, if I have a fiction scene where my characters are hiking in the Alps, guess what? I'll be able to write as though I'm hiking with them, and we will see everything. Just like I did the New Hampshire experience in my novel Voices, which published 12 years after my hike. Our minds and bodies have amazing potential to retain information in all its forms. It's up to us to unlock it.

One of the most observant people I've ever worked with is George Lucas. The legendary filmmaker introduces himself, then promptly scans expressions, gestures, body language and eyes around the table. He partially measures people from particular words they say—and words they leave behind. He zooms in between the lines. For instance, you won't win points with the *Star Wars* creator by uttering "impossible," "out of my reach," or "prohibitive." He developed computer-generated special effects, digital filmmaking and the THX sound system that changed filmmaking and enhanced our theater experience because people told him he *couldn't* do it. Lucas also prefers not to sit at the head of a table. He would rather exchanging ideas and concepts like everyone else. Plus, he knows others will relax and open up more if he joins them. He misses nothing in an exchange, as the detail work in his films suggests. Likewise, great writers observe an object, person, inner feeling or moment to a point where it cannot be observed any further. They run the string all the way back to the spool and release an entirely new expression. Then they present it so the reader can experience what they've experienced.

Perception, inner observation mixed with intuition, concerns your feelings, the dialogue between mind, heart, body and soul. Most of the world focuses on external events and circumstances, disconnected from the tranquil world within, where we find deep joy. And also unlimited creativity. By connecting your outer and inner abilities to observe, you will see ten layers of bark on that river birch tree in New Hampshire and *feel* the sap receding into deep roots for winter. You will move towards a state of superconsciousness, or what poet Li-Young Lee terms, "superabundant presence." Go there. And return—often.

Here's a true story I wrote in a flash fiction format (100 words or less). "Enchantment" took place in the Hohensalzburg, the medieval fortress overlooking Salzburg; among other things, it is a prominent backdrop in *The Sound of Music.* Watch how outer observation, inner perception, movement and dialogue work together:

> How do we escape?
>
> We're surrounded by thousand-year-old stone walls, questions, a midnight moon. I pull on a four-foot-thick walnut door. Nothing. "It's the 21st century, and we're locked in a castle," she says.
>
> We yell for help. Clouds eclipse the moon; a gnarled oak moans, chasing off a white owl. A dragon spits fire from a second-story window. The flames jut ten feet, evaporate.
>
> "Let's go."
>
> Two young women come outside. "We heard you."
>
> "You live here?" I ask.

"Oh, we were bored and were lighting hair spray on fire," one says.

They lead us to the overnight exit.

When an observation or perception moves you, it has the potential to move your reader. When you move the reader, the reader becomes part of the story. From there, we'll look forward to buying your books, feature articles and stories when they're published. Because, they will be.

APPLY & INTEGRATE

- Watch the subject or object of your next observation for a longer period than normal. When your brain first says, "Time to go," take it as an invitation to go deeper.
- Always ask questions while observing; see how the moment will work on paper.
- When observing and writing, jot down everything that comes to mind; don't wait until tomorrow or the day after. You may lose the spirit and power of the observation. Something I heard from a retreat leader: "You will leave here full of energy and inspiration, but if you don't apply it at home, you'll lose 90 percent of the *energy* of being here within a week." Pack your journal along. If time is limited, write sentence fragments or sketch it out; also write down connecting thoughts. Same goes for capturing dreams.
- Read your notes, close your eyes and visualize yourself back at the scene. Allow your natural *state* of superabundant presence to take over. Put it down on paper with full energy and feeling.
- Every day, try to observe something entirely new—or look at an object from a different perspective. Observe with the wide-open eyes of a child. The contemplative wisdom of an elder. The earth-wisdom of an animal. Stretch your writing muscles with crisp verbs and imagery. Pour out your vision for us to see.

EXERCISES

- Practice the "Zoom In, Zoom Out" exercise described earlier in this chapter. Mentally draw a five-foot circle around and above you. Write at least 250 words to describe what you see. Extend out to 10 feet, then 25, 50, 100, writing at each "station." Then zoom in, bringing the circle down to 50 feet, then 25, 10, and five. Compare the difference between your outbound and inbound passages. Practice in a natural setting and in your home environment. Try it in a busy city square. Use the next time you write something new. Make it a "go-to" exercise to sharpen your observation and perception with everything you write.

- Take an hour to deeply observe a man-made or natural object, individual or social setting. Write what you observe. Then, for the next 500 words you write, weave yourself into the moment. Write the piece as fiction, creative non-fiction or essay—whatever suits you. Then edit. Cut away adverbs, unnecessary adjectives, and disparate thoughts. Insert action verbs to emphasize the power of your direct experience. Combine the telescope of observation with the microscope of astute inner perception.

- Write down two or three instances in your life in which you felt a state of superconsciousness, deep mindfulness or superabundant awareness, when everything felt connected around you and you felt connected to everything. In your journal, describe each of these moments in present tense, as though happening now. Recapture their feeling.

- Next time you're in a public place, observe another person (discreetly, of course). Watch their mannerisms, body language, facial expressions, attire and physical appearance. Take your observance inside and write 2 or 3 paragraphs that capture what you think the person is like—characteristics, habits, ways of speaking, interests and how they handle situations. Base all of it on your observations.

Q&A TAKEAWAY

Q: How do I determine my patterns of observation? How can I move from that point towards the heartbeat, or essence, of what defines that object, person or moment?

A: Find a place where you can quiet your mind. The next time you observe something, ask: What do I notice first? Why? What does that lead to? What does it make me think about? What *moves* me within what I observe? Do I return to the same observation? Or jump to something else? After a few such sessions, you'll figure out your observation pattern. From there, every time you observe, drive right to the central question: *what moves me?* Write from that point.

Q: How do I dive deeper into observation so that I can sense the inner life of the object, moment or person, as well as the outer life that I see, hear, touch, feel and taste?

A: The simple answer is *know thyself.* If you know and can identify elements of your inner life—how spirit moves you, what and why you feel in certain situations, the way your intuition works, how it feeds your life or writing purpose—then you can perceive the inner realm of another person, moment or object. My experience has been that if we don't know ourselves IN-timately, then it's impossible to truly know another in that way. Same goes for the people we write about.

Q: What are some of the best moments of "superabundant presence" in my life?

A: What qualifies as a life-changing event? Or a moment that changed how you feel and view things? Do you remember how you felt, what you experienced? Those are your "super" moments—all loaded with great story potential.

Q: How can I transfer that level of perception to everything that I observe—and then write it into my stories, poems, essays and books?

A: Develop a sense of urgency—and then the discipline of patience. When you perceive something that moves you, write down the essence of the experience ASAP. Later, draw it out slowly, carefully, using words specific to the experience, and "feeling" verbs and imagery that speak to the heart rather than mind. Most of all, practice perceiving and writing. Eventually, the two will merge, and it will become second-nature.

SEVEN

Your 12 Senses

Austrian philosopher/educator Rudolf Steiner described 12 human senses, not the standartd five. Explore how the 12 senses enliven and amplify your stories, essays, journals and poems—and put them into action.

"How much fuller and keener is the sense a man then has of his own human nature than when language is merely felt in its abstraction!"

—Rudolf Steiner

I peered wistfully through the window, watching another Southern California summer day saunter past like a *sweet dream, inviting and enticing* . . . but out of reach. Sadly, I was stuck writing online training programs for business leaders, a great *resume gig but* a real pitchfork stuck into this *perfect day.* I grumbled, rubbed my eyes, and returned to my topic: emotional intelligence.

Seconds later, my sweetheart leaned into the room, long hair flying to one side, her rangy six-foot frame filling the door jamb. She held her bodysurfing fins. "My friend just called, and the water's running across the parking lot at Tamarack." Thrill and excitement danced in her deep green eyes.

When the ocean crosses the parking lot at Tamarack State Beach in Carlsbad, our home town, it means one thing: giant waves, pushed further ashore by rising tides. When those tides started to recede, the waves would pitch up ideally. *I might add that the entire eastern basin of the Pacific was under a tsunami watch, thanks to another massive earthquake off the Chilean coast, half a world away . . .*

I'd bodysurfed in a tropical storm, hurricane swells . . . the ultimate surge of wave and energy! No need to ask me twice.

Ten minutes later, towels, water and clothes for dinner packed, we were off. For the next 45 minutes, we bounced up and down like a couple of surf-stoked kids, practically yelling at cars to slide over and let us through. I'm sure the other drivers couldn't quite come to grips with these tanned creatures, both north of 50, acting like they were ditching school instead of taking their grandkids to the beach.

When we reached the freeway, a mile east of the beach, a salty mist hovered like fog. Only it wasn't fog, but detonated sea water, airborne remnants of the wave-bombs strafing the shoreline. Our hearts raced—and our focus intensified. It grew quiet in the car. As lifelong surfers and bodysurfers, we knew that when sea spray filled the air, nothing short of complete mindfulness would suffice. People died when losing focus in an ocean like this.

Finally, we arrived. The waves, normally a few feet high this time of summer, ranged from 10 to 12 feet—big enough to lap against the second story of anyone's home or office building. We both loved challenges that shattered limitations and preconceived notions of, say, our biological ages. Once over dinner in San Francisco, after I picked up Martha from her month-long pilgrimage to India, she told me about jumping off 30-foot cliffs on her 53rd birthday. (Her much better description opens her memoir, A Taste of Eternity). The young, conversative couple sitting next to us, their jaws dropped, probably thought she'd escaped from Langley Porter. A psychiatric hospital. We're just that way. We jumped off cliffs, ran crazy distances, swam in ice-cold rivers and alpine lakes, walked miles and miles in pouring rain . . . and bodysurfed waves you're warned about on TV.

Now, we walked on the beach. Storm surf from New Zealand marched 8,000 miles and unleashed 12-footer after 12-footer a few hundred yards to sea. Inside, I didn't see anything pacific about this ocean, only a washing machine with a nasty rip current. Peligro! Gefahr! Pericolo! Danger! Remember the tsunami watch, Bob? I turned. "Are you sure about this?"

She glanced over, her normally radiant, confident smile clipped to a *slightly* nervous grin. "Let's wait and see if there's anything rideable."

We stood for 20 minutes, about 19 longer than normal, presumably to study the waves. In reality, we were gathering our nerve. Though both excellent ocean swimmers who knew how to plunge under waves to avoid their turbulence, we knew our limits and when to stay on shore. This was a day to stay on shore. "Might as well," she said, *shrugging her shoulders, her grin playful.* "We drove all the way down here."

"Let's go."

We swam out, leaving our common sense and rational reasoning powers on shore. For the next hour, every sense in our bodies, minds and beings stood on highest alert. If we were hooked up to the Caltech Seismological Laboratory, we would have registered a Richter scale reading. If not us, then certainly the ocean. We tried to catch waves, but fell into gnashing pits of water, driving hard into the bottom; Australian surfers call these head-first wipeouts "diving for lobbies (lobsters)." On one wave, I was pinned down head-first for so long, and so hard, my lungs began lurching. Finally, I popped up like a duck, boardshorts half-stripped, legs akimbo. Martha laughed uproariously, though she too was shaking off a slathering in the whitewater spin cycle. We always bodysurfed together, operating on the buddy system, eyes always spotting each other.

We could've written about this adventure by just decribing our body language and eye contact. Leo DiCaprio won *the* Academy Award in *The Revenant*, in part, for conveying that very thing. "He uses his body, which is wounded, and a pair of eyes to convey so many emotions in takes six or eight minutes long," director Alejandro G. Iñárritu said. "He makes us believe that he is cold, that he is wounded, that he is devastated, that he is angry, that he is hopeless. Without one word, we understand what this guy is thinking and feeling."

Sounds to me like the perfect recipe for not only writing experience, but writing readers into our experiences.

Meanwhile, I coughed out a mouthful of sea water, the sand within it gritty against my teeth. "What—a-a-are you . . . laughing about?" I panted.

"What idiots we are for thinking we have control out here. *Mother Ocean will eat us for lunch.*" She laughed harder, a far more nervous laugh. The laugh of someone a bit afraid.

The next set roared in. We got clobbered by a half-dozen waves, caught inside, in the "impact zone," each wave feeling more like a punch to the head than a bucolic beach outing. After we tumbled underwater like rag dolls, I threw up the white flag. "We're going to get too tired if we stay out here," I said. *And drown.*

She agreed. We swam parallel to the shore to avoid the nasty rip current, which raced northward like a shoreline river. Finally, we found an opening and bodysurfed to shore, a half-mile north of where we started. Later that night, after showering, dressing and enjoying a wonderful sushi dinner, we walked to the nearby pier. It was packed with gawkers, tourists and locals alike, watching the giant surf explode, the spray hitting onlookers 20 feet above the water. Mobile devices fired away. It looked like a rock concert.

I turned, the very sturdy pier shaking slightly beneath us. "I can't believe we were just out in that," I said. Actually, I yelled: the roar of the sea drowned out anything less.

She broke into her mermaid smile, serene and calm, the afternoon already tucked into her bones and cells. "I'll bet we're still talking about this years from now. We're crazy."

The next day, I prepared a writing workshop. Still buzzing from the vibrational fury of this old man's foray in the sea, I thought of the senses we'd engaged. I mentally rattled through my checklist of 12 senses that Austrian scientist, educator and anthroposophist Rudolf Steiner laid out, later to become core curriculum at Waldorf schools in the U.S. Life/well-being. Touch. Balance. Movement. Smell. Taste. Sight/vision. Thought. Speech/language. Hearing. Warmth/temperature. Ego/the other. I was familiar with Steiner's findings. Besides proving a thorough way to assess ourselves and our relationship to the world and each other, they changed the way I wrote. (Notice how several have two qualities—one an outer quality, the other reflective of our inner state of being). I could animate characters like never before, and see new things in my own life, the way I navigated it, and how I perceived my surroundings, inner and outer.

What I realized is that, like writing itself, our senses are about relationship. They are our physical and intuitive antennae, the connective tissue that affixes our bodies—our sense vehicles—to our spirits, souls, psyches, impulses and actions. The more attuned to our senses, the richer and deeper the resulting experience. The five senses we learned in the early grades give us the basic story, which can be encyclopedic in itself. But twelve senses? It's like jumping from black-and-white silent films to 3D.

Yet, senses offer us the easiest way to engage a reader. Good writers do it through the reader's senses, too. Once the reader is fully involved, you can unfurl the full scope of your work. This is why 90% of all opening scenes in books and movies are dramatic and filled to bursting with sensory experience.

How do we write with the senses? First, we understand and assess the senses as they define our relationship with our bodies, minds, and world. Following that, we can ask questions, write them out, and acquaint ourselves with . . . our deeper selves. It's almost like doing hatha yoga, and holding the posture for its deeper benefits, rather than settling for mere physical flexibility exercises. Then, we can use these to enliven any person or character at any time. Here are the 12 senses, with identifying and prompting questions to carry forward through writing:

- **Life/Well-Being:** Is your subject happy? Sad? Downcast? Upbeat? Show the sense of well-being with a glance, a comment, a posture. "If I remember right, on the other side of that rock is a wonderland." Clearly, Megan has a strong sense of well-being.
- **Touch:** Use your characters' or narrator's fingers, arms and even cheek-nuzzles to reach out and grab your readers. Touch with your words; help us feel what you feel when you write the piece.
- **Balance:** Balance can be conveyed as physical, emotional, mental or spiritual balance. Are your characters balanced in their lives? Their actions? Their way of walking? Convey balance (or lack of) through the way characters describe or perceive their world.
- **Movement:** How does a person move? Upright and rigid, or with knees bent in a loping gait? Hurriedly, sluggishly or with calm focus? This speaks volumes about one's inner character, level of stress, and can also be used to pace a story. Read an Elmore Leonard book; his crackpot capers, such as Get Shorty and Rum Punch (which became the movie Jackie Brown) are built on character movement and dialogue.
- **Smell:** Smell is the most primal, and the unsung hero, of all senses. It offers direct access to old memories and dreams, the readers' own olfactory sense, and a place of instant focus and presence. Nothing enlivens a moment—or a piece of writing—like a well-placed scent. It is the highway to the feminine point-of-view and its

softer, deeper, more mysterious insinuations. They walked past fern-covered forest floors, muddy bogs and freshly sprouted mushrooms, their noses feeding on the moist pungence of creation. When we travel, we remember the scents and smells as much as our visual experiences. When we attached scents to those experiences, well, that moment will become forever accessible to you.

- **Taste:** Think of taste not as "salty," "bitter," "sweet," "sour" or "astringent," but as a vehicle of association—"the orange tasted like a swampy Florida grove." Also, taste refers to a preference for a particular style, set of activities, or word or music choice. When you, your subject, or character tastes something—food, drink, the air, "the sweet taste of victory"—share it with us.
- **Sight/Vision:** What you see and how you see it are critical. You are the eyes of your stories, books and articles. Your vision is myopic, binocular and monocular, all at once. We see nothing without your guiding pen. Steiner went further, however: He described vision as a sense. What are your aspirations? Your dreams? Your visions? They color the other senses; they often define future life choices. Trust the images that come to you and take us deep inside while continuing to unfold your essay, story, poem or journal vignette.
- **Thought:** If you're a writer, you're good at thought—maybe too good. For many, the biggest challenge is to get "out of my head" and not become overly analytical or intellectual. Use thought to describe your subject's mental world and its possibilities and limitations. Show how characters work their way into and out of decision-making situations. Also, thought includes memory and how it serves the moment.
- **Speech/Language:** Rarely do we think of our speech as a sense, but it is precisely that: The sense of how we communicate what we see, what we think and how we feel. Prior to white man's arrival in North America, there were 500-plus Indian nations, all with different languages and dialects. I contend there are still 500-plus specific dialects here, regional and local. That's just for English speakers. Taken further, I believe there are 7 billion distinct ex-

pressions of speech and language—one for each person on earth. We cobble together pieces of slang, vernacular, idiosyncratic phrasing, colloquialisms and accents from everyone that touches us in some way. Whispering, yelling, even-voiced talking and whining also convey different experiences. What is yours? Show this in your dialogue and in the way you set up conversations. Show it in your own voice.This includes interior dialogue, the unspoken thoughts between words.

- **Hearing:** Hearing incorporates the sounds of the world and takes us into the inner worlds of our characters or subjects. Give us insight into their favorite music, the sounds around them, and how they experience and react to those sounds. Write about the sound of a quiet seashore. Then write about a honking horn. Feel the difference in your body tension, word choices, way you write and present your description. All of this came from what you heard. Hearing and touch are also the senses that produce the best action verbs, which move your narrative along.
- **Warmth/Temperature:** Some people are "hot-blooded;" others are "cold-blooded." What characteristics do you associate with these descriptions? Gain the measure of one's sense of warmth and temperature: Is your protagonist a snow sports fanatic? Does the Upper East Side debutante flee to Florida in the winter? Is the room warmer or colder when someone walks in? Do they perspire in public? Fold their arms together and act cold when asked a personal question? All of these little "tells," to use a poker phrase, offer great insight into our relationship with our surroundings and our selves—perfect for conveying experiences.
- **Ego/The Other:** Is your character or subject confident? Arrogant? Depressed? Self-absorbed? Concerned with others? Dutiful? The sense of ego/the other is the sum total of a person's characteristics. You can show this by writing yours or another's actions, or thoughts—and then showing the reaction. If someone criticizes you, do you flinch? Crumble? Embrace it? Fight back? Each answer conveys an entirely different experience.

APPLY & INTEGRATE

Steiner's 12 senses can and probably will change the way you write, observe, research and even live. It's one of the greatest tool chests for story development and observation I've found. They were revolutionary when Steiner introduced a century ago; they are just as revolutionary now.

Study the 12 senses as they thread through your life, and as you perceive and associate with them. Make this a regular activity in your journal, or blog. Do yourself the great favor of being able to write each sense, inside and out. As writing gifts go, this is one you can give yourself with a golden ribbon and diamond ring on top. It is that precious. Once you attune yourself to such areas as balance, thought, movement and ego/the other, as well as the other senses, your perception will expand. So will your perspective. When I got the hang of this, I felt like an NASA astronomer looking at the first deep-space Hubble images after being limited to backyard telescopes my whole life. The leap in perception is that profound.

Pick up one of your favorite novels, memoirs, non-fiction books or books of essays. Go to a chapter, read through it, and see how many of the 12 senses you can identify. Then, go back and study how the author used verbs as vehicles to convey those sensory experiences. Now, integrate your own 12 senses into your writing by using action verbs that trigger the senses. Does she move? Or does she dance, slide, flow, boogie, lope, saunter, sway, or glide? Each sense opens a treasure trove of synonymous verbs. Create a list of verbs for each sense. This will be your initial aid for writing about the 12 senses.

EXERCISES

- Create an incident or situation that requires complete presence in the moment. Or, recall a perilous or momentous incident in which your complete awareness was required. Write about this experience as though you are living it now. Show us everything you see, everything you feel, how you or the character moves or responds from there. What are the surroundings like? What sensory perceptions do you have? Write 1,000 to 2,000 words from the center of the experience. When you're finished, go back and see how many of the 12 senses you incorporated into the piece—and how many descriptive verbs you used to drive your piece.

- Try a simple exercise in cross-sensory perception, or synthesia. What does a gravel road *sound* like? What does a desert in July *taste* like? How does a mountain *balance* itself (hint: think of earthquakes, volcanoes and mudslides as physical and emotional expressions)? What does a baby *hear or say inwardly* in its silence? What do puffy clouds taste like to a circling eagle—or you, as you're watching the eagle? Write one-paragraph answers to these questions. Take one, and expand that paragraph into a short essay or vignette.

- Capture a moment in which you felt heightened—perhaps a vacation highlight. Write about it. Within your description, devote one sentence to each of the 12 different senses. Study the difference in your perception; it can be almost as profound as looking at a crowded nightclub from 12 different points of view. See how your perception and experience changes with each sense.

- Go into your kitchen and smell your favorite spice. Really inhale and let the scent take hold in your brain, and follow the feelings and/or memories it stirs up. (For me, a sprig of sage lands me directly at the aspen tree lines of the Rockies.) Go online and quickly read up on their history, how and where they are gathered, ancient uses, what they trigger in the body, health/medicinal benefits, etc. Write down what you experience, interweave some of your flash research, and see how many senses are perked by this simple act.

QUESTIONS FOR FURTHER DISCOVERY

- Observe a person or a group of people and analyze their senses of balance and movement through the way they talk, walk, move around a room or street, and use body language. What do these movements tell me about the person's style of living and how they operate in the world?

- How do I express the 12 senses in my life? How can I more fully express and identify the 12 senses so that they become familiar to me?
- What are some of the ways in which I can electrify or deepen my writing to become more sensual; to write from the senses in a way that captivates readers?
- What would happen if I incorporated the 12 senses into the way I write about my dreams, observations or travels? In what ways would this expanded form of writing change my work—and my life experience?

EIGHT

Accessing Your Inner Stories

We carry thousands of stories within us. How do we tap our memories and hearts, and weave the emergent stories into our writing?

"Storytelling is an excellent way of caring for the soul. It helps us see the themes that circle our lives, the deep themes that tell the myths we live."

—Thomas Moore, author, *Care of the Soul*

What happens when we attend family or school reunions? After introductions and a trip through the buffet line (or after dinner), we seek out pockets of relatives or classmates, mingle—and "talk story," as Hawaiians call it. Someone shares a reminiscence, another adds to it, and then something is said that triggers a memory you'd thought long forgotten. It rises like a subterranean, your mind already whipping it into story form before the words leave your mouth.

This was certainly the case in Summer 2015 at my family reunion, the first time in 60 years an organized reunion had been held—and the first time ever that members of all three branches of the Yehling family joined together. Since I was not alive yet in 1955, my older cousins treated me to a healthy dose of Bob stories. My father. Such as, how he snuck behind his parents' back to play high school football, became a star—and his father found out while listening on the radio. Busted. Or, how he helped his large family during the Depression by doing yard jobs or hauling waste, paid for in chickens and eggs. He was seven or eight, and the baby boy in the family. My brother, sister and I have been hard workers since we were seven or eight . . . part of our inner stories. Now I knew the source.

Soon, those stories drew a dozen reminiscences, all headed in the directions of the tellers, who often closed their eyes, and accessed poignant, heartfelt moments that made you laugh, cry, or think. Each account triggered more stories the tellers thought were cast adrift with adolescence, or a forgettable moment. As an author, I listened and thought of the chain reaction, fomented by one well-told, deeply felt story. It was like the Big Bang at warp speed. Each story gathered new strength and detail, a new rendering, fueled by its nucleus—the experience, event, or conversation we embedded in our bosoms.

Reunions always have reflective, thoughtful, heartfelt, happy and sad phases. We catch up with old favorites and create new friendships, moving and shifting with, well, our lives and the stories that define them. These can also lead to hilarious encounters. Many years ago, I traveled on the press junket with the NFL's San Diego Chargers to Oakland, to cover the Chargers-Raiders game. The night before, two fellow sportswriters and I milled around the hotel conference room area, bored. One saw a sign: the Oakland Tech High School Class of 1957 was celebrating it's 25-year reunion. He was in his early 40s, the same age as the alumni, his youthful face set beneath a full head of prematurely silver-white hair. "Let's crash the reunion," he said. "We can pull it off."

"How?" I asked nervously.

He looked at the other writer, about 10 years younger, and me. I was 20 years younger. "Bill, you're my little brother tonight. Bob, you're my son," he said, the devil appearing on the stage of his pupils like a rock star. He gave me a stern look. "Don't step out of line." He slapped my shoulder and laughed. "Let's go."

He plunged into the room, trailed by his two reluctant accomplices. For an hour, my colleague held court, a master storyteller regaling his "classmates" with tales that rattled from his tongue like tone poems, one experience after another, full of life, cadence, action and drama. He told stories like he talked sports, stretching bounds but lacing every sentence with accurate detail that kept you right here, right now. Great BSers are also great storytellers; his circle of listeners kept growing. The other writer and I played along, nodding our heads, eating from the great food spread, saying things like "yeah, it's true."

Finally, one of the reunion organizers realized that we were impostors, party crashers. But fun crashers. As soon as our colleague's cover was blown, he turned to us. "Go. Into the lobby. Now. Move." We escaped, laughing uproariously.

Later, I asked him, "How did you convince them? And keep them convinced?"

I'll never forget his answer. "Same age. Same cultural references. Same experiences in high school, really, felt the same things, liked and hated the same classes, listened to Elvis and Jerry Lee. I just switched the location. My stories were their stories, deep inside. They just kept coming out."

While he fictionalized settings for the ruse (and the wonderful free meals), his response opened my eyes to how stories work, and how we retrieve and present them. That night, I also realized how and why our stories connect with readers, even though they are our stories: Because they hit at the heart and soul level, at that universal place we all access. When we can reach inside ourselves and grab those always shy, often frightened denizens of our cells and bones, or grab the feelings that escort them into the light of waking consciousness, we can present material that instantly grasps the mind and heart of our readers. Those stories speak to the most fundamental, primal aspects of who we are. They become "A-ha!" moments, when we find a sentence, quote, revelation or statement that feels specifically written to us.

How often do writers mix their inner stories with their subject matter? All the time. It's not only the point of this book, but also a vital means of conveying authenticity and animating the narrative, no matter the form of writing. By scanning some of my favorite writers, I see Joyce Carol Oates' brooding, mysterious 1950s upstate New York adolescence in many works. What is John Irving's masterpiece, The World According to Garp, if not a mixture of inner stories and his wonderfully dark humor and imagination? Do you think Isabel Allende could write her juicy anecdotes in House of the Spirits or The Stories of Eva Luna if she hadn't lived in Chile or attuned with the supernatural, endemic in Latin cultures? The great Paddy Chayefsky, three-time Academy Award-winning screenwriter, created from his own persona his most memorable characters, Howard Beale of Network, and Marty, the woman-shy butcher that became a Best Picture recipient.

How about Lois Ehrdrich, whose novels drip with Native American practice, ritual, and struggle, every story filled with nectar, many laced or originated from stories buried deep inside her. Of course, all great memoirs require constant contact with our innermost selves to succeed.

So, how do we do this? How do we access our stories? We trust our deeper selves, the 90 percent beneath or above our waking consciousness, to deliver the goods. As Italian filmmaker Federico Fellini noted, if you remember something, it contains your truth—and no matter what you write, it carries that truth. Obviously, that truth is vital to non-fiction writing. Fiction writing also revolves around truth—the more you tap into universal truth, the more believable your characters and stories will be. "Good writing is the result of sweat, hard work and a belief in truth; truth as a condition of the human heart, not the individual human heart but the composite heart of man. A good writer must be able to see that truth and believe in it," William Faulkner said.

I will add that, when we access one of those stories and their truth(s), we find a path, or chain link, to another story—or an entire nest of our own past moments. The way to contact, re-experience, and record them is to go to them. With few exceptions, they will not readily come to you at first, an exception being dreams. If something triggers a memory, see if you can latch onto the memory and see the story surrounding it. Write it down. Keep writing. Don't stop, even if it's difficult. It always opens up more avenues. As my friend and former newspaper editor, Bill Missett, told me years ago, "Grab a story or thought, and think it all the way back to its origin. Then feel it. Then write it." He used that very process to write the wonderful Awakening the Soul trilogy.

Many of us grew up on legends, myths, and true stories that stood the test of time: The Bible, The Epic of Gilgamesh, Greek and Roman myths, The Canterbury Tales, 1001 Arabian Nights, and The Voyages of Sinbad the Sailor were among them. Perhaps the oldest are the Vedas, the ancient Indian stories and scriptures. In full form, the Vedas contain more than 100,000 verses that were memorized and orally transmitted for countless generations until stone tablets and papyrus came along.

I see the Vedas as an allegory to ourselves. I'd like to think that each of us has 100,000 stories tucked within our cellular and intellectual memory banks. If only we can get to them . . . The challenge is to sit down, write, and keep the internal censor turned off. Don't let your rational, present-day brain and its halting thoughts into this process. Gain access to your deepest self, let the memory fully flower into story, and go with it, as though it were a series of hiking trails you'd never walked before. Explore. Discover. Be present. Write. Maybe you'll arrive at an essay; maybe a short story. Maybe today's journal entry will wind its way into a novel or memoir ten years from now. The key is to bring your stories above surface, into the light, onto the page.

Another thing to consider when accessing inner stories: People love to read about people. They want to know what makes others tick, their fantasties, secrets, mysteries, motives, loves, triumphs, scandals . . . in other words, what joins us as well as differentiates us. If someone picks up your how-to book on gardening, or cycling across the state to raise money for cystic fibrosis, then share with them your first memory of working a garden, or your emotional interaction with a cystic fibrosis victim that triggered your desire to write. A client, of mine, Dr. Madeleine Randall, dove into her memory bank and case studies—all of which are also *her* stories, being the attending doctor—then wrote a hundred anecdotes and inserted them into *Soul Doctoring,* a great look at how medicine can work in many different ways, shapes, and practices. As one certified in 18 different modalities, from Western medicine to Ayurveda, Traditional Chinese Medicine, Native American shamanism, and others, Dr. Randall laid out her amazing inner stories as well.

If you're prepared to write, and prepared to receive *yourself,* without self-critique or interruption, then the stories will appear. In my novel *Voices,* I recounted a moment when the protagonist, a rock vocalist, grabbed a temporary roadie's cell phone during a concert and serenaded the roadie's wife (who was on the phone) and 50,000 people at the same time. A touching story, a nice bit of fiction. Except the original story was true. Marty Balin of Jefferson Airplane was the vocalist, I stood next to the roadie, and tears filled the man's eyes when Marty handed him the phone after serenading his wife (and the 50,000 others) with "Miracles," his mega-hit from the mid-1970s. When I wrote a concert scene for my novel, I had no idea the cell phone memory would surface, but it did. I closed my eyes, let the memory take me back to that day, to that story, felt again the roadie's shock and elation, peered into Marty's owl eyes, and wrote the *feeling.* That is where our inner stories and our readers' minds intersect.

APPLY & INTEGRATE

When we open to our collective experiences and stories, and dive into our innermost stories, we reach those places where readers instantly relate to the writing—because our feelings trigger their feelings, shared on a page. Our thoughts trigger their thoughts. Be specific and focused. Let the storyteller within, your Muse, sift through available options to present the story inside . . . then go in and grab it. Along these lines, it becomes more vital to write journal entries, letters and short essays on a regular basis. The more you do so, the more fluid and clear the road between your working mind and your soul, the eternal storycrafter. Eventually, you don't always have to reach in and grab a tough-to-access story. It will *appear,* in a strange alchemical way, and it will trust you to carry it forth, as you will have done many times before. Practice not only makes improvement, but it also opens creative channels. Keep yourself creatively loose. Finally, trust that you will receive exactly what you need. When we trust, our stories will populate and animate anything that we write—in the measure needed.

Also, notice above how I continuously prefer to use the word *feeling* rather than *emotion.* We often merge the two, in both description and action, but they are quite different. Consider them opposite signs of a coin titled "intimate experience." Emotion is reactive, a behavior triggered by the moment itself—happiness, sadness, anger, quietness, moodiness, ecstasy, depression, etc. A million triggers stir our emotions, but the emotions themselves are actions taken in a specific moment. Once they dissipate, new emotions dive in to replace them. We feel emotions as hot or cold, sharp or soft. On the 12 senses scale, they are all about warmth and temperature.

Now let's flip the coin. Feelings are emotions after they've taken root and grown within us. They draw the emotional charge into our bodies, then grow into little gardens of context, perspective, depth, purpose, and meaning. We might get charged up emotionally about a new song, but only when we take it inside, touch and feel it, and connect in that way to its melodies, harmonies, rhythms and lyrics, do we become *inspired* by it—at which time we'll never forget that song. Nor its inspiration. How do we know? Every time it comes on the radio, or we stream or play it on our mobile device or stereo, we *feel* the emotional content of the song, as if hearing it for the first time. Feelings can last forever.

The easiest way to draw this contrast is by looking at one of the two most written-about feelings in history: love. How does love start? With attraction, desire, and, let's be honest, a fair bit of lust. To me, "love at first sight" is a bit premature. It's "intense desire and attraction at first sight," an emotion, a red-hot chemical reaction between two people. When that reaction starts to dissipate, the emotion either grows roots, deepens, expands, and connects the two people with love—a feeling hard to contain, because it's within and outside of us. That can happen two weeks, two months, or two years later; we all have our love stories. Or, it dissolves into nothing, and we wisely retreat from each other like spent waves receding to the sea, deepened by our experience together, gathering ourselves again for the day when the feeling of love does visit us. If I wrote "love" as a story, or book, Chapter One would feature the intense, all-senses-in, exciting period of meeting and getting together, sparks flying through the air—and bodies and hearts. From Chapter Two forward, it would be a much deeper read.

Emotion is like that—the tip of the iceberg. Feeling is the 90 percent beneath the surface, the good stuff, what drives you when writing. When readers feel what you're feeling, then they not only read your writing, but *experiencing* it.

So, when you're accessing innermost stories and presenting them, readers are picking up on the emotions and feelings—instant connection. You, on the other hand, are writing from the feeling, which has universalized your initial emotion and given it context, perspective, depth and meaning within you.

A few things to remember:

- Our stories are our greatest source material. They are the greatest chronicles of our lives, more authentic than photographs and certainly more authentic than the opinions or descriptions of others.

- When we write our own experiences, we feel everything. That feeling breathes life into characters and scenarios, and serves as the intersection point to the reader's attentive reading mind.

- All it takes is a smell, a sound, a word . . . and our memories are triggered. When it happens, find something—anything—and write the story down. It is your truth, waiting to be shared.

- The subconscious mind always lobs memory balls to the surface. Grab them and write them out. If a sentence triggers another memory, keep writing.

EXERCISES

- Create a fictional story, or a fictional aside to a friend's story. Or your own. Reach inside yourself, and try to remember moments or stories from your own life that directly relate. Or idle dreams and fantasies. For example, if you've dreamed of becoming a gourmet chef, write about serving up exquisite dishes for a monarch—and integrate your favorite cooking experiences into the chef's *inner feelings.*

- Write a 1,000-word essay, short-short story or narrative sketch, taking a story from your past and placing it in your life today. How differently do you see the world? How much does that story shape the world through your eyes today? What about that past story *applies t*o the situation, or the way you are, today? Bring the reality of life into the mix. As *The Right Stuff* author Tom Wolfe says, "The genius of any writer will be severely handicapped if he cannot master, or if he abandons, the techniques of realism."

- To access your stories, write down a memory. Now, free-associate by surrounding that memory with 5 to 7 experiences or sensory memories linked to it. Write a paragraph from each of the experiences—and see if they trigger additional stories.

- Call up a story from your adolescence. Imagine you are telling the story to someone. What would you say? Write it out as dialogue—see where it takes you.

- In your journal, write down everything you can remember from the most incredible/successful/difficult year of your life. Or, a smaller period filled with peak moments. Hold onto this list: It contains the most electrically charged story cels in your being. All you need is a thought, memory, certain smell, sound, taste or sighting to trigger them. Get those stories down!
- What one event caused an irrevocable change in the course of your life? Identify it, and write 2 to 3 paragraphs about how your life changed—or 20 to 30 pages. Write as much as you can.
- Write an open letter to the storyteller/Muse within you, asking for stories and experiences that relate directly to your current writing. Give this letter pinpoint focus. Be specific.

QUESTIONS FOR FURTHER DISCOVERY

- Once I access the memories of my life experiences, how do I differentiate what truly happened from what I am re-creating as part truth, part fiction?
- What are some of the ways to write about events of childhood and adolescence, particularly dialogue, when it is impossible to remember every word that was spoken?
- What is the emotional charge of this story, or piece of writing? Can I describe them? At what point do I carry my characters' (or my own) emotion deeper, into feeling?
- What did I love most about the legends, myths, fairy tales, adventure or love stories my parents, elders and mentors told me? How do my stories connect to the deeper messages of these tales (hint: they do; just need to discover the connections)? What *feeling* does that bring out in me?

NINE

Refined Storycrafting

Use your life experience, skills and imagination—and techniques like social media micro-blogging, "hangtag stories," book reviews, letter writing and flash fiction—to refine your storycrafting skills.

"I'm gradually learning that, paradoxically, it's the blunderings, giving ups, breakdowns, in spite ofs, chance encounters, letting gos, and mess-ups, that have led to most of the creativity in my life, not the "enlightened" inspiration, and certainly not feeling in control. It's the listenings, buzz hums, the falling (leaping) down the rabbit hole, the stepping through the looking glass, barefoot, with no suitcase, in new territory."

—Susan Wooldridge, author, *Foolsgold*

In 2013, I spent time in Maui working with Clay Marzo for my book, *Just Add Water.* Clay is an anomaly, a world-class surfer who is autistic. Quick: how many autistic world-class athletes do you know of? It won't be a large number. I flew over to tape his story, interview others, immerse in his environment, and see how he lived his daily life.

My immediate challenge: Clay doesn't talk a lot, especially when the subject is *recalling* something. He never takes it beyond a few sentences at a time. When you're trying to write a 90,000-word book on a living subject uncomfortable with speaking or making eye contact, you need to find alternatives.

I dove in. Literally. Clay thrives in the ocean, where he operates with his greatest power, confidence and expressiveness. He is a maestro on a surfboard. For my part, I spent quality time bobbing up and down on a surfboard, letting his surfing and unique relationship with the sea tell his story as well as words ever could. While watching Clay perform his wave-riding magic from my front-row seat, I noticed things I never would have seen on video or from shore, even from 50 feet away: How he uses his hands to feel and "read" the rhythm of the ocean, or, as he puts it, "reading the lineup." It described, non-verbally, his uncanny ability to deduce how little bumps would jack up like spooked stallions to become waves. How he paddled into the wave parallel to shore, rather than perpendicular, the customary way. How he read the ocean better than most oceanographers and practically all meteorologists. And, most of all, how his presence changed from social and physical awkwardness on land to, well, that of a sea mammal. As his behavioral therapist, Carolyn Jackson, told me, "Most surfers paddle out to catch waves. Clay paddles out to *become* the wave."

That's what I saw, too, enough to open *Just Add Water* with:

> The pristine waters off Maui's west coast convey majesty and presence fitting for the ancient Polynesian Sport of Kings. They are about to be stirred by a tall, angular magician with a swimmer's build and moves that very few on earth can match. Every time Clay Marzo enters the Pacific – nearly every sunlit hour of every day he's not traveling, if the waves cooperate – he paddles out to commingle with his soul, which seems to breathe with gills. Waves come to him as if silently summoned, enabling him to turn around, drop in, and unleash rides so dynamic, outrageous, daring and graceful that you're left grasping for superlatives. He speeds through waves like a dolphin, explodes off the top like an attacking leopard, inverts and bends into impossible positions like an Olympic gymnast . . . and always seems to land on his feet. Like a cat.

Had I not paddled out, hiked volcanic rocks to secluded spots on Maui's rugged northwest coast, or plunged fully into his experience, the second half of this paragraph would not exist. It speaks to something I long ago realized about writing and, in particular, my career track: Direct experience tells the greatest stories of all.

When we write our life experiences, one implication might be that we're looking at things *we did.* The first half of this book focused on bringing past experiences into present light on the written page. However, as writers, we need new, fresh material—and what better than the action, emotion, feeling, and value of continually experiencing new things? Or finding fresh new expressions of the familiar?

I've spent my entire career bent on experiential writing. It traces back to one of my favorite authors, Jack Kerouac, and his "stream of consciousness" approach: everything is happening right now, in present tense, every bump and turn, every groove of development in our character. *Carpe diem* and writing are not strange bedfellows, but soulmates. I adopted this approach at 17, creating a career in which I played lunar rock catch with the third man to walk on the moon (Apollo 12's Pete Conrad), screened movies with George Lucas, paced at ultramarathons, hiked and trekked in the world's great mountain ranges, toured with legendary musicians, tried bronze sculpting with an NFL offensive lineman, exchanged poems with former President Jimmy Carter . . .

Point is, my resulting chapters and articles could have been constructed with rote research, phone interviews and observations of others. However, I wanted my readers to feel the magic, the motivation and inspiration behind my subjects. I wanted them to feel like they knew the people or places, intimately. I wanted them to take my subject's hand (or my own) and take the journey *together.* I would be a guide; nothing more. These are departure points for my writing. To achieve them, I always seek to experience . . . and bring my digital recorder or a journal at all times.

How do writers directly experience? Same as everyone else—except our eyes, ears, senses, bodies and minds morph into radar systems that pick up *everything.* Good, attentive writers can and should be as deeply sensitive as autistic children, who, by the way, pick up things well beyond our everyday perception. By working, playing, creating, recreating or partaking actively, we not only have the experience, but *immerse into the world that forms it.* This is critical. The more we can recreate the setting, mood and feeling that we directly experienced, the more effective our writing. This goes for drop-in sentences as well as entire books. In the passage from *Just Add Water,* one reviewer said, "I was in the ocean with you on the first paragraph." How? When I wrote it on a computer, and the reviewer was sitting in her office in Manhattan? I wove my direct experience into the sentences:

- *He paddles out to commingle with his soul, which seems to breathe with gills.* I watched Clay's face physically change from tense to a Zen-like calmness, and, from ten feet away, I *heard* his breathing drop to almost nothing.

- *Waves come to him as if silently summoned.* He closes his eyes, wiggles his hands in the water, and feels the impulse of the sea. Invariably, within moments, a wave pops up. He says nothing when he does this. You can't see these hand movements from anywhere but right next to him.
- *He speeds through waves like a dolphin.* Many times, while surfing or bodysurfing, a porpoise or dolphin has popped up. After gulping, and making *very sure* the dorsal fin was curved and not triangular (signifying a shark), I've watched them bodysurf beside, ahead of, and even a few inches beneath me. Dolphins and porpoises glide like eagles when they ride waves, in complete synch with the current and pull of the wave. When Clay races along a wave, before blasting one of his signature moves, he glides just as serenely and smoothly.

The most important point about continuously filling your basket with new experiences? The stories often write themselves. No longer are you telling readers what happened; you're *showing* them. That's the biggest single difference between successful and unsuccessful writers and authors. When we rely on others' comments, research and passive observation alone, we're forced to tell the story, because *we haven't felt the direct experience.* By not feeling directly, we lose connection with mood, atmosphere, and the tactile sensations that fill our lives and keep us coming back for more. Sure, in our jobs or everyday life, we write many things that are not borne of direct experience. This ratchets it up to the next level—the level that drives you to bookstores seeking good reads. The more you direct experience and put into words, the more you, too, will *show* the story, always an inviting proposition for a reader. Maybe you organized a $50,000 crowdfunding campaign. I never have. I want to know the inside details of setting one up, the thinking process, which I could never adequately portray, even if I interviewed you. But you would portray it fully, because you lived it. You would be writing from direct experience.

I'll give you another quick example. Recently, I attended the book signing of Lita Ford. In rock music circles, Lita is a goddess—not because of her looks (though that definition would certainly apply), but because she plays guitar like no other woman in rock & roll history. She was the lead guitarist and driving force of the legendary 1970s all-girls rock group The Runaways (the movie *really* did her an injustice), then wrote and sang with Ozzy Osbourne on Ozzy's one and only No. 1 hit single, "Close My Eyes Forever." She's in a league of her own. Lita and I grew up 60 miles apart in Southern California. We're the same age. We did the same things as kids—went to the beach, made mischief at school, listened to hard rock music. We got into our careers at the same time, at 16. Two years later, when I first interviewed her backstage, we were on opposite sides of the same coin: She performed rock music, and I wrote about it. Now, she was an author, sitting for the first time at a featured author's signing table—a place I've occupied a few times.

When Lita and I talked, we didn't need cultural introductions. We tuned in to each other's backgrounds, and built from there. Because we shared many experiences, we had other things to talk about besides "saw you at the Whisky-A-Go-Go, Golden Bear and Bacchanal in 1978." Our direct experiences took our conversation to a richer level.

Likewise, when you can embed or detail your experiences to the extent the reader feels they know you, then your writing can really soar. That is when you get past the "back story," and into the substance. But to do that, you need to tune into your experiences, mundane and spectacular alike, and ask yourself: How did it enrich me? Change me? Change my perception? Lead to something bigger? Impact my values/opinions/plans? Make me happy? Or sad? Improve (or not) relationships with others? Help or teach? Inform? Show me something new about myself and my potential?

These are questions writers need to ask of their own experiences, because our goal is to build a narrative from them that will connect with readers. Questions like these are the little bridges that get you there. As my friend, the *Poemcracy* (now in its 26th printing) and *Foolsgold* author Susan Wooldridge wrote, "I'm gradually learning that, paradoxically, it's the blunderings, giving ups, breakdowns, in spite ofs, chance encounters, letting gos, and mess-ups, that have led to most of the creativity in my life."

They also lead to writing that readers can't resist.

As children, our worlds consisted of the loose, spiraling, boundless structure similar to, well, a well-woven story. Wonder why journey stories captivate us? Because they *are* us; they speak to our most primal tendencies to wander, travel, reflect, dream, explore. We did this routinely as kids. A dozen endings seemed possible. Riveted, we could not be interrupted. We were terrified, electrified, sad, joyous, inspired and taken on flights of fancy all at once. Think Grimm Brothers, L. Frank Baum, Peter Barrie, Carolyn Keene, Dr. Seuss, Madeleine L'Engle, Lois Lowery, J.R.R. Tolkien, J.K. Rowling, and even Stephenie Meyer knew this? Of course: They knew precisely how to mix magic, innocence and wonder, how to tap the primordial storyteller within all of us. They appealed to our experiences, and to our aspirations for greater experience.

We are born storytellers. We're genetically hard-wired: that gene has been in our primal DNA since our deep ancestral forbears painted hunter-gatherer picture-stories in France's Chauvet cave. Now, as working and aspiring writers, we're bards for our times, chanting verse and painting pictographs. The rhythms lie within us.

A key to good storytelling is to *listen to how the story wants to express itself.* This involves what we've discussed so far—opening up to the Muse, making past experiences available, outlining and preparing, and "living with" characters or story in our heads for weeks or months—or a minute, if it rushes out—before touching down on paper. But in my experience, the story expresses itself much more boldly, confidently, and fully if it draws direct from our activities—*especially* a fresh activity. One action can trigger a hundred memories and a hundred possible next steps, all at once. What could be more magical than that? Fact is, were storytelling a planet, this place of molten inner creativity would be its core.

Another key of good storytelling is a quality I've mentioned before: Trust. We *must* trust ourselves to open up fully, put everything down, and embrace the results. We can edit later. Trust that your story will spread itself and go where it wants to go. Trust that it can and likely will *lead* you on a twisting, winding path that eventually returns to your original destination—with many spices and jewels collected along the way. Trust that you're *the best person* to write it. Trust the character (or inner) conversation, narrative, similes and metaphors that flow through you. As prolific novelist Henry Miller wrote, "What is an artist? He's a person who has antennae, who knows how to hook up to the currents which are in the atmosphere, in the cosmos; he merely has the faculty for hooking on, as it were."

Indeed, when we're writing, everything around us seems to take on an elevated life of its own. If we trust, we become instruments and communicators. Trusting storytellers operate in superconsciousness, in a state of conscious superabundance. It's a similar state to what we experience after meditating, praying, or experiencing something uplifting or awe-inspiring. I'd like to be there 24/7! In this place, we observe things differently, more deeply. We see new gradations of color, or design, in an object we've viewed a thousand times before. We dive into the vocal ebb and flow of someone's words, rather than half-listening to "idle chatter." As a very wise Vedic author, Patanjali, put it 2,500 years ago, "When you are inspired by some great purpose, some extraordinary project, all your thoughts break their bounds: Your mind transcends limitations, your consciousness expands in every direction, and you find yourself in a new, great and wonderful world."

When you find your voice, your unique vision-experience-language-style of telling a story, readers will gravitate to you.

Which leads to the final question: how much of your personal experience do you share in each of your works? Another, more specific question to drill that down: To whom do you tell and write your stories? Your perceived readers? Your family? A fantasy lover? People on the other side of the world? Kids you teach? Yourself? That's up to you. A great perspective comes from *House of the Spirits* and *Eva Luna* author Isabel Allende, a fiery, wise and passionate woman, just like her stories. Isabel imagines herself surrounded by a small group of adults and children in a tiny village. She makes sure they're comfortable, and she tells them a story. She takes them back home—to their deepest roots.

And we keep turning the pages.

APPLY & INTEGRATE: Lessons from Social Media Messaging

In order to hold the reader, a story must be catchy, informative, enlightening and engaging. These days, it also must be quick: You have about as much time to engage the average reader in your piece as do people posting on social media sites. In other words, not long.

I have a "workout" I like giving writers. Think of a story you want to write (or are writing). Now, see if you can write its essence in the following formats:

1) Facebook Post—give yourself 100 words max.

2) Micro-blogging—Respond to a Facebook post with a 50- to 150-word description of your story. Also, micro-blogging offers *great p*ractice in briefly and succinctly tying personal experience to any number of subjects or issues. I micro-blog all the time, as it provides good promotion *and* sharpens up my writing for book projects.

3) Hangtag story—Imagine your piece is an article or line of clothing, and you are conveying the message on a hangtag (50 to 100 words). How would you sell it—and share the essence of the story? Great hangtags are those that tell creative stories about their brands—quickly. It's a great technique to know.

4) Book Review—Write a review of your own piece (250 words or less). Focus not so much on what is good or bad, but on the storytelling qualities: did you share the experience as you wished? Is it rhythmic? Strong? Capitvating? What is the takeaway from the story?

5) Twitter Post—How would you summarize your story in 140 *characters* or less?

6) Flash fiction—Boil down your piece into a 100- to 200-word miniature of itself. See that it has a beginning, middle and end, conflict, resolution, and at least one defining character or narrator.

This is a robust workout, akin to assigning my high school cross-country teams hill interval repeats on a hot day. What it does, though, is boils down your story to its core, its essence, the place where your direct knowledge and experience intersect with the craft of presenting it. It also carries a secondary benefit: You will need to become skilled at these forms of communication, anyway, to be able to promote your work at the ever-important P2P level (peer-to-peer). They are key to book sales and promotion in the 21st century.

Working your story to its bare bones, and then extending it, leads to story*crafting*, conveying your experience with a specific technique, style, and voice. This takes practice, a lifelong practice; I've been practicing storycrafting since I was eight. I still study books, authors, attend readings, talk to authors, professors, artists and musicians, and go to oral storytelling festivals, all to refine my skills, to pick up a technique or a turn of phrase, then mash it up with my voice—the trailhead of my life experience.

Above, I mentioned a great "boot camp" practice to develop storycrafting skill—flash fiction. Try writing one flash fiction every other day, for a week. Or a month. This is what coaches know as "deliberate practice," aiming every action, no matter how apparently inconsequential, toward the goal outcome: in this case, successful storywriting. Take a *recent* direct experience, write a powerful first sentence, and tell the story. Then write stories about anything you can think of, and see if you can weave in a bit from your own personal knowledge of the subject.

A parting note: writing practice should never end. We're much like classical musicians, performing or visual artists in this regard. The more you practice, the more proficient you become. Not many of us are as fortunate or focused as the 17-year-old high school junior in New York City who wrote a 2003 urban fiction bestseller, Twelve. I've heard guesses as to how many words—in all forms—we produce between the time we learn to write and when we find ourselves proficient storytellers and storycrafters. A common guess is one million words. That's *4,000* double-spaced pages! I definitely feel that *Outliers* author Malcolm Gladwell's figure of 10,000 hours to attain skill mastery is in the ballpark. That is one year of 24/7 writing, plus 1,200 hours. Or, more realistically, a few hours a day for many years. Storycrafting is a measure of continual practice and improvement as much (or more than) than raw ability.

EXERCISES

- Recall a cherished moment from your childhood or adolescence. Write about it in 500 to 1,000 words, invoking a feeling of magic, innocence and wonder so that *you* feel under the spell of the moment again. (If you do, your reader certainly will, too.) When you're finished, tell the story from another character's point-of-view. Note the difference in direct experience and connection.
- A modified flash fiction exercise: Write down three events in your life. Tell the story behind one of the events in 200 words or less, including conflict/resolution, plot and a main character.
- Take the other two events, and tell the story of each from a different point-of-view. In one, use the first person "I." In the other, use the third-person "he" or "she," stepping outside yourself to relate the tale.

QUESTIONS FOR FURTHER DISCOVERY

- What new twist can I use to turn my stories, or the stories of others, into pieces that enlighten, entertain and/or grab the reader so they won't let go?
- Do the ways in which weave and thread through my stories reflect the *rhythm* of how I experience things? If not, what am I missing? What happens if I incorporate that impulse, or inspiration, into my story?
- When I was a kid and a storyteller shared about his/her life experiences, and turned it into a story, what did I like the most? About the delivery, approach, substance, storyteller's voice? Where can I add that to my writing?
- When I tune into the heart of a story, what am I hearing? How am I connecting it to my personal experience? How would I write that story were it my own?

TEN

Your Journal, Your Writing Lab

Our journals are diaries, confidants, and sources of tomorrow's memories. They are also chemistry labs to test ideas and polish our craft.

"The simple act of journaling allows us to examine our beliefs, desires, and hopes; exult in our celebrations and excise our sorrows; and explore the changes we make – or don't make – in our lives."

—Barbara Stahura, Author,
Brain Wreck & After Brain Injury: Telling Your Story

A little more than a decade ago, my dear friend, author Barbara Stahura, was sitting at home in Tucson, AZ when she received the news that her husband, Ken Willingham, had been gravely injured when a sedan turned left in front of his motorcycle. He had no opportunity to avoid the collision. Ken's worst injury was a serious traumatic brain injury. For weeks, she kept vigil at the hospital and rehabilitation center, wondering how much of the man she knew and loved would return to her. It took years and much hard work, but thankfully, Ken made the most complete recovery imaginable from such grievous injuries.

The accident changed Barbara's life, in more ways than one. Already a prolific journaler, she wrote her way through her painful, sometimes frightening time as Ken's caregiver. Diagnosed with secondary traumatic stress soon after the accident, she found healing and comfort in the practice of writing down her deepest thoughts and feelings about what was happening.

In 2007, having realized the therapeutic power of journaling, she created a journaling program for people with brain injury and began presenting it regularly at a rehabilitation hospital in Tucson; her husband was among her early participants.

One thing led to another. First, Barbara published a memoir, *What I Thought I Knew,* which included a chapter titled "Brain

Wreck"; she later developed the latter into an e-book. She then teamed with Susan B. Schuster, M.A., CCC-SLP, her husband's speech therapist during his recovery, to write *After Brain Injury: Telling Your Story; A Journaling Workbook,* of which University of Texas professor James W. Pennebaker wrote, "This is a beautifully written and thoughtful book that should be embraced by anyone who deals with the aftermath of brain injury."

Barbara wasn't done. Inspired by the courage and honesty of the people in her groups, she wanted to become the best journaling facilitator she could. In 2009, she became a certified instructor of Journal to the Self®, a journaling program created by Kathleen Adams, founder of The Center for Journal Therapy. Then she took the next step and became a Certified Journal Facilitator through the center's Therapeutic Writing Institute. Now living with Ken near Evansville, Ind., she has since taught and spoken nationwide, in the process becoming a respected and sought-out facilitator of various journaling programs. (For more, check her website at www.barbarastahura.com)

Where did this begin? With ideas Barbara sketched out in her journal, fueled by her husband's recovery experience and her desire to help others trying to understand their new, post-injury selves as much as possible. In so doing, she married her vast writing talents to a higher purpose . . . and the results speak for themselves. And, I might add, she did all of this after turning 50—when many of us wonder how we can possibly shift gears and try something new.

Our journals can be anything we want—diaries, confidantes, travelogues, collections of little stories, sketchbooks, chronicles of major experiences in our lives. To a working writer, however, the journal becomes something else. It is the place to flesh out new ideas, run story lines through different perspectives or points of view, write about new experiences or subjects, recount conversations, try new words and structures, and work out the myriad problems that pop up while writing stories, articles, and essays. Many learn to write deeply in their journals, freed from the intrusion of others to explore the frayed edges of hurt feelings, or to plumb deepest emotions, impulses, fears, desires, and life situations. In fact, when we abandon our inhibitions and let our souls and hearts take over, deep journaling becomes transformative (more on this in Chapter 11).

In short, our journals are not only chronicles of our lives, but also our creative and psychological gold mines. They are also our chemistry labs as working writers.

Take a look at the way you journal today. (If you don't journal, now is a great time to begin). Ask yourself: Do I write diary entries? Do I explore the subject a little more deeply and thoroughly? Do I sketch out new adventures and experiences? Do I share my feelings? Do I capture conversations and friendships?

What do I write about?

Now, imagine your journal as a chemistry lab. Or a gold mine. Or, to get closer to the heart, your *alchemical* lab. Your three essential tools are in place: Pen. Journal. Mind. (Or, computer and mind, for computer journalers). In front of you is something to write about. Will you simply write a description? Or experiment, and try to write from within the center of the experience? Or use new verbs to drive the narrative better? What about that conversation you had or overheard? How can that fit in? Is there a way of writing that impresses you? What if you practiced that technique until it fused with your voice—and out came an entirely new structure no one has ever seen before?

That's how the journal works as a chemistry lab. You use it to literally mix new concoctions of subjects, words, people, voice, narrative structure and styles that, when practiced, often transform your writing. By doing this, you not only become a better writer, but also a more versatile writer. Like an athlete, your flexibility increases, then your dexterity, and with it your ability. Hear the phrase, "move mountains"? That's what happens when you journal with the mind of a working writer. And when those mountains move, out come the veins of gold: stories you never knew were inside you. Figures of speech, verb choices, similes and metaphors that leave you almost as breathless as your readers. The ability to write about anything, at any time. Quite frankly, your journal is the key to the kingdom of your greater writing potential.

I've journaled for almost 40 years. I started off writing a glorified diary, but soon realized I could use it as my chief tool for expanding and improving. One year, I committed to writing about a different subject for all 365 days. So, today, I feel comfortable writing about anything—and can switch between subjects in a heartbeat. Many of my friends think this is natural. The only natural aspect is my *willingness* to be versatile. Another year, I focused on how writing heals—and then used it to work through some personal issues that were blocking me from writing with greater emotional depth. Now, I can get right to it—whether it's my deep heart matter or a fictional character's. Or, an article subject's. It took me several years to break out of the objective structure of journalism and into the subjective realm of fiction—and I have all the "experiments" that show the slow transition. Now, I love writing fiction as much as non-fiction. All of my books and ghostwriting efforts gestated in my journals, as well as another two dozen ideas that may or may not see the light of publishing. Going back over all 40 years, I have quotes, snippets of writing style, observations, and phrases of more than 500 different authors, filmmakers, musicians and artists, every one of which I studied at some point.

Therefore, my journals are creative messes. They are full-on adventures in the sandbox. I've got sketches, doodles, encircled words, memorabilia from concerts or showings I then wrote about, arrows and lines shooting from page to page, author quotes taking up entire pages, and thousands of different topics, written as diary, letter, poetry, lyric, dialogue, flash fiction, short stories, character sketches, and anecdotes. My journal reflects my working mind, always popping with ideas, thoughts, ways of connecting apparently separate topics or words. It is all fueled by the one maxim I live by, best described by my good friend, 1970s-80s figure skating legend and author Tai Babilonia: "Everything is possible. Always." When it comes to writing, that is true for all of us. We just need to realize it. Journals can be our best friends in making that happen.

The other thing about journaling as a working writer concerns *location, location, location.* Write on-location whenever possible. Many days, it might be your writing nook, desk, patio, or while snuggled with a coffee or tea on the sofa. However, get out and write in different places. Capture the place within your journal entry. How does it feed you? What are its features – and charms? What do the hills, valleys, creeks, sand, mountains, or ponds reflect in you? What kind of story is trying to come out as you sit there? For this reason, I always dateline my journal entries (a newspaper term to show location of a story, i.e. "INDIANAPO-

LIS, IN—"). If I see too many consecutive datelines that are the same, I find another location and write there. This practice not provides a regular helping of fresh air, but also enhances our ability to write perspective, point of view, setting, and variety of subject.

I've written in caves, boats, planes, storage rooms, museums, galleries, rock concerts, beaches, mountains, cabins, castles, stadiums, forests, and so much more. Just the nature of this list breeds diversity, variety, adventure, discovery. By journaling in countless locations, I can now close my eyes, envision the location, and write directly into it. And capture a character's, or my own, relationship to that place.

APPLY & INTEGRATE

There are a number of core journaling practices that serve writers well. Here is a checklist of simple steps to turn your journal into the chemistry lab that will start revealing your deeper literary gold very, very soon:

- Journal every day, or at a minimum, two to three times per week.
- Find a comfortable place that feeds your creative mind. Write there.
- Read what you just wrote. Add to it, change it, see what ideas for new writing spin from it.
- At least once a week, write "on-location," away from home.
- Every week, bring in a sentence or paragraph from a writer you admire. Analyze it in words, work it over, then practice writing *from* (not in) that style. Marry it to your normal writing voice.
- Every time you journal, pick a vocabulary word you love to read (or a new one entirely), but have never used in your writing. Write a few sentences with it. The next time you journal, intentionally use the word in the flow of your entry. Do it again. Embed that word into your written

vocabulary. (This works extremely well with verbs, and breaking out of that impersonal, passive academic and business writing style so many of us carry.)

- If you're researching an article, book, or work-related matter, write about your research. Experiment with approaches until you're comfortable. Then you're ready to bring it to life.
- Add a couple of lists to your journal, things that also reflect your walk in life. My lists include books I've read (have them all, over almost 40 years), films I've watched, music events I've attended, and new places I've run.
- Write at least one page per sitting. Try to write more. Always stretch those muscles, extend, try things with words you've never tried before.
- Think of your journal as your inner universe, brought to paper, always expanding. Then expand your bounds, daily.

EXERCISES

- For your next 10 journal entries, write about something entirely different. Study how well your writing style, and description, carries from subject to subject.
- Take an unusual or particularly beautiful word that makes you buzz inside (mine is *synethesia*). Play with it. Try it in sentences. Experiment with including it in a letter, article, short story, or essay you might be writing. How does it add life to your writing?
- If you're working on a life story or based-on-my-life piece—memoir, autobiography, series of letters, blogs, self-help articles, etc.—take your next subject into your journal and flesh it out. Challenge yourself to dive to the deepest place within yourself to bring out the fullest essence and substance of the passage. Write sentences that startle, shock, or compel you to go further. Don't worry if they don't flow out the way you thought of them—it's a journal. You can scratch out and try again.

- Journal about your previous day, but in this format: What happened? How did it make me feel? What was the next thing I did, my next action? What did I do differently? How did I feel? What happened next? This draws setting, actions, feelings, and narrative together, and is a great tool for personal experience story writing.

QUESTIONS FOR FURTHER DISCOVERY

- After reading today's journal entry, what new thing have I learned about myself and how I experience things?
- What 10 words or phrases have I always wanted to incorporate readily into my work? How can I structure my daily journaling so I can experiment with and apply these to my writing?
- Which author(s) leave me with fullest anticipation? Whose works do I feel like I'm *drinking* or *consuming when* I'm reading them? What about their voice, material, or style turns me on? How will I use my journal to develop my own ability from their example?
- In looking at my journal entries for the past several weeks, or months, how have I changed as a writer? A person?
- What can I do to expand my range and reach? What is out there that I want to write about, but have never tried?
- What styles, words, stories, perspectives, vignettes, anecdotes, inner discoveries, or observations in my journal can I incorporate, now, into my writing?

ELEVEN

Writing the Tough Stuff

Personal experiences include the most difficult events in our lives, the moments that change, forge, and transform us into who we are today. When we write about them, we can heal ourselves—and impact others' lives.

"Expressive writing changes us. It brings peace to our hearts. It restores balance. Writing connects us to the parts of ourselves that have been lost, abandoned, neglected, forgotten, or ignored. We learn that there are wise, friendly, and sensible selves within us that want to succeed. They are willing to share their wisdom with us."

—Kathleen Adams, author, *Expressive Writing: Foundations of Practice*

I faced an inner crisis. I spent the second half of my twenties rising like a Phoenix from some poor choices, working furiously for five years to build what stood before me: marriage to a beautiful woman and soul. A beautiful daughter already showing her enormous musical talent. A thriving writing and PR business, built mainly on great surfing beaches, mountain resorts, and triathlon courses in Hawaii and the U.S. mainland. A gorgeous four-level home on 2 ½ wooded acres. Annual hikes to different mountain ranges. Great health, great friends, and real success. What a great scenario to blow out those 30th birthday candles at a surprise party, complete with my favorite musical theme—the Sixties!

Everything was in place for a great life. However, lurking deep inside my soul was an angry, brooding inner child, a self-saboteur, one quite capable of throwing a tantrum and eradicating all of the above. It happened a year later, when my perfectionism, workaholism, negative childhood messaging, intense self-created pressure, and old addiction patterns went *tsunami* on my willpower.

During the ensuing despair, I awoke from a troubling dream: a red-faced, bug-eyed tyke of about ten screamed at me, "Tell my story! Tell it now! I want my voice back!" He jumped up and down in a sandbox, kicking and flinging sand everywhere, finally blasting my eyes with a handful—

I woke up with a start, rubbing my eyes. My heart not only pounded, but hurt, as if someone just opened it up. *Tell my story! Tell it now!*

I started writing. For the next six weeks, I "listened" to this petulant troublemaker inside spewing his anger and fury over incidents two decades in my past. I wrote what I felt, which was a very large voice overpowering me and booming through my chest. *If only my fiction characters would do that!* I thought.

The result? A novella-sized work entitled *The Child Speaks Up*. The narrative arc was quite clear and concise—a locked-up child seeks its freedom of full expression, and then promotes the idea of being heard always, in quieter, more subtle ways. First, it needs to be released from its iron shackles and prison, to be free to see the world through its childlike eyes again. The end of the story was far lighter and joyful than the first part.

If a breakdown, epiphany, catharsis, anxiety attack, and revelation can all happen simultaneous, then it happened at this moment. I sat against the wall, hyperventilating, the past six weeks of speed writing opening up my chest as effectively as a heart surgeon. The child's voice was my own, speaking from the place I buried it when I was 12. For a variety of reasons, I became dead-serious at that age, concluding I could no longer operate like a kid. I barely survived being 13, began working at 14, married for the first time at 21, had my daughter at 23, crashed and burned at 25, and had it all at 30. Only to lose it again.

One thing I didn't have, though? Inner happiness. The angry voice, now on paper, told me why: Because I'd left my inner child in the cold, damp shadows of my difficult adolescence, and with it, my sense of humor and ability to make light of the world. Everything I did with utter seriousness, life and death, as if it were my final act on earth. And I never stopped working: I did not want to feel inside.

The Child Speaks Up never went further than a single raw draft. However, I went further, reclaiming this voice, giving it space, and unlocking levity and light in my heart and soul. I began to feel magic, innocence and wonder again, celebrating the mercy and beauty of every moment, cracking jokes or seeing the humor in situations, mixing my eternally intense work practices with fun and play. I also began interjecting humor and the now-playful inner voice into my writing, which transformed the mood and tone of most of my work.

A quarter-century has now passed since the child spoke up. Now, if I told any friends I've since made that I was a dead-serious, perfectionist workaholic who rarely smiled, never laughed, simmered with an steady, unremitting anger, and felt like doom and gloom would visit him the second he lightened up, they'd wonder what I was smoking. Which I would take as a compliment: things have changed.

Things changed because I was willing to write the tough stuff, the hardest moments of my life.

I was willing to write, day in and day out, while feeling the full force of the pain, suffering, trauma, struggle, despair, and even brief suicidal ideation (at 13) it triggered. I was willing to hyperventilate, struggle for breath, shed many tears, relive specific moments, write my anger like a cat clawing out of a bag . . . and then reach in, grab that snarling inner child, hold and nurture it, and let it speak. I lost weight, skipped many meals, pulled all-night witching hour sessions like Anne Rice, and got that damned little kid out of my system . . . only to welcome a beautiful inner child that continues to serve me well every day.

It is difficult to write the tough stuff. That's why it's tough. Yet, this emotional content is precisely what drives readers to your work, buyers to bookstores, and millions to therapists' offices. It is part of our blueprint as human beings, our purpose in life: to experience, learn, heal, and grow. It is part of the duality of life: light and dark. Sun and shadow. Up and down. Happy and sad. Only, it's the tough side, the pieces of our lives and souls either stuck or lost in the black holes, shadows, nooks, crannies, and sinkholes of our innermost selves. When we feel such pain like this, we also feel an existential threat; we protect ourselves so it doesn't happen again. We do so by building walls, and wearing armor and chains, constricting our hearts, limiting our life experience, and stifling our emotions and ability to transform through the situation. We do so again and again . . . anything to kill the pain. And we don't think twice about it. *All in all, it's just another brick in the wall.*

Yet, the tough stuff sells. Whether sharing problems with our friends, or presenting them in book form, we find a ready audience. We also find it far tougher to shake the negative events and emotions we carry inside. Why is that? Well, it's for the same reason. During a mindfulness class I took, the instructor, therapist Robin Smith Stutzmann, said, "It takes an average of three minutes for something good that happens to us to stick, to become part of us. And it sometimes flies away. When something negative happens, it takes three seconds. And it seems to stick forever."

Stick . . . interesting word. When we write particularly sticky content, material that readers dog ear, underline, memorize, or otherwise hold onto, we say that material is *resonant,* or that it *resonates* with the reader. Putting its musical connotation aside, *resonate* can draw from resounding, loud, catchy. However, it comes from the same word root as resin—thick, sticky substance. When people write about difficult challenges, dark moments, it resonates with readers because it sticks to their minds, hearts and souls. Remember what Robin Stutzmann said about taking three seconds? It doesn't take much longer for us to be hooked into such a story, *especially* if it connects with unresolved feelings inside us.

What happens when we write *through* the pain? What happens if we tie our minds, hearts, and words together, tear down the walls, unhook the armor, and bust the chains?

I'll give you a great example. Years ago in a "Writing to Heal" workshop I taught, I was approached by Pauline J. We had just finished an exercise in which I instructed participants to write directly into the part of your body that is giving you discomfort. By doing so, we can often drive down to the source of that discomfort . . . then the emotional connection, and even the spiritual link. Western medicine focuses on diagnosing and treating systems. The Ancient Ayurvedic system of India treats symptoms as the final and most superficial of seven levels in which dis-ease (note the hyphen) progresses from inception to physical manifestation. I developed this exercise with the Ayurvedic approach in mind.

Pauline walked up, tears glistening from her eyes, her smile radiant. *Odd combo,* I thought. "I just want to tell you that this exercise just broke a dam inside my chest."

I love a good compliment. "Thanks. What did it break through?"

"Everything I've held to my chest these past years. My feelings. The pain of my divorce. Moving forward. Loving again. My will to live."

My will to live. Those last four words carried extra weight. "How did a 45-minute exercise connect with your will to live?"

She showed me her piece. She wrote a short, snappy conversation between her two breasts, in which they act they're cleaning out an attic, ridding themselves—and the heart between them—of the hurts, abuses, heartaches, shutdowns and other constrictions that threaten their way of life. "We were once so full of ourselves, talk of the beach. We had our guy who loved us. Then he ignored us. Then he hit us. Then he cheated on us. Then he hated us. Now we don't even want to come out again. We're keeping it close to the chest."

Your jaw on the floor yet? Mine was, too. I fought back tears as I handed the story back to Pauline. "You've got a book here," I said softly. "This is one of the most amazing things I've ever read."

Pauline rubbed her eyes. "I have Stage 3 breast cancer," she said. "I held this stuff in my chest too long, and it got me. Tonight, I realize it all has to come out."

"Because you held things close to her chest."

"Not any more."

Pauline continued writing after the session. Eventually, she wrote a series of magazine articles, and even discussed a book. When I heard from her again a year later, she'd just returned from a week in Hawaii with her new love, her kids were thriving in school, and she was happy. The best news? Her breast cancer was treated and gone.

When we write about our ailments, traumas, challenges and travails, we open ourselves to a pool of feelings and emotions we *don't* want to face. Sometimes, they feel like an endless swim in blackness. Others, they feel like a slow disappearance into quicksand. Nobody in their right mind *wants* to plunge into that despair, yet millions read self-help books, novels, memoirs and advice columns, or listen to songs to connect with your experience, and see how you dealt with and (hopefully) emerged from it. Not only is our writing therapeutic for us—"the one-cent-per-hour psychiatrist," a famous writer once quipped about deep-self writing—but it is also therapeutic, life affirming and quite often life-changing for others. I can't think of many more reasons to bring out our stories than to touch others, to make their own walks through life more purposeful and manageable.

There are a few key points about this kind of writing:

- Start with a story. If you can start by writing a story about something that happened to you, *and then* dive into how you felt, responded or reacted, you will find it easier to "enter" yourself.
- Write from the center of the pain or struggle. Give your issue a name and a face. Make it a character if necessary, as I did the inner child. Write the world of feelings as it exists from "the eyes." Use Steiner's 12 senses to paint a sensory picture.
- Write with metaphors and similes, to make it easier. "My pain was black ink mixed with super glue." Or, "I hobbled like a football player hit once too often." When you make these connections, they give strong pictures to yourself and readers, and enable you to move forward.
- Attach your feeling or emotion in the moment to every sentence you write. Describe the setting or situation, then dive into your experience, your feelings, your perceptions. Use "I" a lot.
- Pivot from problem to solution. When describing traumatic, difficult moments, it's important to see the flip side—the solutions and opportunities. Write about the positives, the solutions. Write the outcome (or desired outcome)—then use it as the destination when you're trudging through difficult writing.
- Plumb deeper . . . and deeper. The deeper you write, the more it resonates with readers—*and the better you heal.* Go as deep as your will and emotion will allow—then stop for the day. Resume from that point the next day. Write until there's nothing left to say.
- Come up for air . . . and share a laugh. What makes us, as readers, continue circling back to even the darkest stories, like *Angela's Ashes, The Glass Castle* or *She's Come Undone?* In all cases, the writers took us from dark scenes with a lighter paragraph or passage—or they told a joke

or delivered a funny aside. In real life, we often break off emotionally tough situations by changing the subject, talking about a lighter topic, or cracking a joke. Narrative imitates life.

- Use your journal. Test-drive your writing in the privacy of your journal. Work with your feelings until you feel comfortable writing about them. Try numerous approaches. When comfortable, bring onto paper. (NOTE: I'd like to mention that a journal, or diary, should never be seen by another—including a loved one, spouse, or friend—unless he or she has your specific permission. Your journal should be a sanctuary, where you can experiment, divulge, or purge in absolute privacy.)

One of my favorite essays is "Fallow Time," by Barbara Stahura (with whom we visited in Chapter 10). Then in her 40s, she sat in a most uncomfortable place, her social life, creativity and inspiration as fallow as an Indiana cornfield in January. Plus, she'd ended her PR career to focus on freelance writing, which, as freelancers know, is a rollercoaster ride between the heights of good assignments and the valleys between checks and acceptances, which can seem Challenger Deep. She dug in, brought her sorrow to the surface, and wrote deep, touching essay.

A year later, she met the man who became her husband. Think one had to do with the other? I sure do. Now, 15 years later, she's happily married, the author of three books, and one of the top journaling workshop facilitators in the country. She told an inner story that resulted not only in more stories, but, as far as I'm concerned, energized a life change as well.

Know how they say the toughest or most determined efforts lead to the greatest outcomes? It certainly holds true when writing the tough stuff. Barbara endured one of the toughest places for any woman—*why does no man want to be with me? What am I doing with my career and life? How am I going to move forward with purpose?* She wrote from the center of that anguish. However, she also wrote from a hopeful place, focused on the rhythms of spring, how yesterday's fallow field is today's bounteous meadow, or harvest. She used her essay to shift her anguish from that dark, sticky, inescapable maw of broken feelings and bones, to what could lay ahead if she *just stuck it out.* Through tenacity, guts, tearful sessions and willpower, she wrote this gem of an essay. Today, looking back, it also reads as a blueprint to emerging from her cocoon, and opening the wonderful life she lives today.

Here is an exercise that can deliver the same outcome. It's perhaps the most powerful writing prompt I've ever used, one that belongs in every writer's quiver of creative arrows. Whether you're dealing with an emotional upheaval, loss of a loved one or friend, physical challenges, or being stuck in your career or life, "Peeling Back the Layers" is how writers like Pauline, Barbara, and others get to the core of their own lives and present it in a way that touches lives . . . and helps heal their own. This exercise can take a half-hour, or last for days . . . up to you. Here's how it works:

1) Write down a single event that hurt and caused change in your life—either suddenly or gradually. Write the event in a single sentence.
2) Write three or four actions or occurrences that preceded that event. Then write something that happened *because of* that moment.
3) Write 150 words from this point, focusing on the circumstances.
4) When finished, read your 150 words. What is the most powerful sentence, the one that stands out? Underline that sentence.
5) Write 150 words from your newly underlined topic sentence. Dive into the deeper layers now. What happened? How did it make you feel? How did you respond/react? What happened next? Show the cause-effect, even if you're only describing your breathing growing rapid out of fear.
6) When finished, repeat Step 4. Then write another 150 words from that topic sentence.
7) Continue repeating this sequence for a few more rounds, until you find you have nothing left to say.

When I first learned this exercise at a writer's conference, presented by memoirist and teacher Lisa Dale Norton (*A Hawk*

Flies Above, Shimmering Images), we did four rounds, or "generations." I couldn't believe how much my original sentence had transformed into the deep, raw, thoroughly potent paragraphs now in front. By drilling down, I'd reached both the essence, or origin, of the issue—and its point of transformation. Since, I've peeled back the layers many times, finding this my favorite go-to "writing workout" whenever I'm getting ready to write memoir, fiction, or helping others with their memoirs. If ever one multi-faceted exercise existed for getting us into deep space to write our tough stuff, this is it. Its creator, Lisa Norton, used it to emerge among the living—and the healed—after being raped and left for dead in a New Orleans street.

APPLY & INTEGRATE

Few writing subjects offer more versatility and diversity in the way we express ourselves than our "tough stuff." Look around any bookstore, and you'll see memoirs, self-help books, novels, biographies, sociology, psychology, poetry, essay, and other titles wrapped around the same theme: *what happened to me? And how can I rise above it?*

Likewise, the way in which we integrate and weave our most challenging moments provides versatility all its own. It's up to how dexterous we are as writers. You can write entire books, chapters, essays, letters, journal entries, thread in paragraphs or sentences laced with your experience—or even embed your most emotionally or physically taxing moments within character dialogue or fiction narrative. By doing so, you enrich the emotional quality of that passage, because the sentences or paragraphs laced with your personal experience instantly give the words energy and realism. When you write with that resonance, readers will follow.

Let's practice this. Take an event that forced you to make a fundamental change in your life, either temporarily or permanently: a broken leg. A divorce. Moving to another country. Communication breakdown with your teen. Rising from addiction. Getting married after being single your entire life. Write a few paragraphs, using the "Peeling Back" exercise shown earlier. Be sure you get beyond surface features and into the meat of the situation. As you carry on with your week, incorporate a sentence, paragraph (or more) of this experience into:

- A letter
- A journal entry
- A paragraph or sentence of a story or essay you're writing
- A blog or micro-blog on the subject
- Entry on a LinkedIn discussion group or Facebook page
- A poem or song
- A novel or narrative non-fiction book you're reading (just pretend you're the author, and write into the story)
- A "Dear Abby"-style advice column
- The first scene of a play—or (sigh) reality show
- The conversation (dialogue) of a fictional character

Keep practicing ways to "drop in" snippets of your life into these and other writing avenues. Do this often. To me, this exercise is like hitting golf balls: the more you practice your swing, and the right kind of force and touch to apply to each "ball," the more refined your swing will become—and the day will come when you can "hit" any "shot." That is the goal.

EXERCISES

- Create a map of a traumatic experience. Put the experience in the middle of a sheet of paper. Now, surrounding it, write out the way you felt, the chain of events that occurred because of that trauma, and how you ended up where you are right now. See if you can organize that map into a cohesive pattern, a narrative arc.
- Write a letter to yourself about this or another event that shook you to the bones and forced you to make a fundamental change in your life. Go deep, immediately: write from within your heart, within the distress. No matter how tough it feels, stick with it. Write with words that invoke feeling, bring back the moment. Read what you've written, and see how you might apply it to your work.
- Expand that letter into an essay or blog, broadening your scope to show how others have dealt with the same or a similar situation. Give an example outside your life. Then infuse that example with the *feeling, perception,* and *thoughts* welling up inside. Do the same with another example. Practice making statements and using your experience to empower the essay.
- Write the outcome. Write an essay about the successes in your life today—then draw us back to the "taproot," a particularly challenging moment that prompted you to change something that set you on your current path. Show not only the challenge, but how you handled it and what you discovered about yourself along the way.

QUESTIONS FOR FURTHER DISCOVERY

- What are three things in my life that caused me to take stock of myself, heal within, and move forward? What would I write about them?
- What strengths and skills did I develop from dealing with a traumatic episode or a loss? How would I break them down if I were writing a recipe for overcoming these situations?
- How often do I journal about my deepest feelings? What would happen if I journaled those feelings—and then wrote a picture of life *beyond* them?
- If I were to write a letter to my most troubled self, what would I say? What would I offer as a way to get out of that jam, knowing what I know now?
- When I read personal challenge memoirs, what qualities and characteristics of the author/narrator keep the pages turning? How can I adapt those qualities in my own life? Where do they fit into my writing?
- When I look back at something I wrote years ago, during troubled times, what do I recognize and not recognize about my self back then? What has changed?

TWELVE

Finish!

The world's file cabinets, closets and attics are filled with half-completed manuscripts. Why were they never finished? Ways to keep the motor running strong for a book or writing project, featuring secrets from literature's best "finishers."

"Writers do not reach the finish line by picking at their manuscripts, circling back, and picking again . . . they dig in, silence the world around them, and GO."

—Robert Yehling

Few things exhilirate us more than finishing major tasks or projects. Our human spirit is indelibly tied to finish lines, and the promises they deliver. We set goals to reach them, focus harder on projects to get there, and celebrate in myriad ways when we arrive. Then, for those who often see finish lines as gateways to larger achievements, we re-set ourselves for the next endeavor, bolstered by the emotional electricity and confidence of our just-completed effort. We live for finish lines at work, in sports, with getting our kids into college, with causes or projects, and with our hobbies. They are the high jump bars of our life, always there for us to scale. Question is, how high or low do we set the bar?

Given our love of reaching finish lines, and the lives we build by achieving goals, why is it so incredibly difficult to finish a book? How and why do we often pour weeks, months, or even years of our lives into preparation and research—and life experiences, start writing like thoroughbreds bursting from the gate of a Triple Crown race . . . and then skid to a stop three, four, or five chapters into our story? Why, then, is it next to impossible to pick up the project in mid-stride and continue pushing, coddling, cajoling or nurturing it to the finish line? And isn't finishing the first draft of a manuscript no finish line at all, but a *beginning*? How can we want to go on, or push ourselves forward, when we've laid our brains and spirits out and written hundreds of pages—only to realize we probably need to rewrite and revise, over and over, to bring it to the polished final shine that ends up on bookshelves? Or magazine racks?

For many years, I was mystified by this apparent twisted dynamic—and a non-finisher as well. It took me awhile to figure out how I could knock out goals and achievements in a variety of areas, but in my most passionate life pursuit—writing—I never seemed to get there. Eventually, when the thick fog of thinking I knew it all finally passed at about age 35, two things dawned on me:

1) Writing (and art, and music) requires complete commitment of body, mind, and soul, *as well as the willingness to bare everything.* Or, standing before your audience naked, as poet Robert Bly put it. How many people can feel vulnerable enough to open themselves up completely? Knowing you might well be sharing this with readers in your community, region, state, country, or the world? And then keeping those soul- and heart-gates open for hundreds of pages and many months, or years? Those are tough questions!
2) Writing letters, journal entries, brief articles, blogs, and other short pieces are akin to running sprints. Magazine articles, essays, and short stories resemble 5K or 10K races—medium distance runs. However, books are like marathons.

In 1999, that last realization grabbed me hard—just in time for my 40th birthday. After telling myself as a small kid and teenager I'd write books for a living, I looked at my work. I'd penned thousands of newspaper and magazine articles . . . but where were the books? Well, no less than a half-dozen partially finished manuscripts sat in my closet or on my computer. One completed raw draft joined them; I never pulled it out for a rewrite. In other words, I lived in abject fear of crossing the finish line with the very work for which I'd spent 25 years preparing as a journalist and magazine editing.

Then I started distance running again. I set goals and milestones, got myself into shape, and ran (and won) some races. Three years later, I decided to aim for a goal I'd coveted since I was a high school runner—competing in the Boston Marathon, the oldest and most prestigious road race in the world. However, I had to qualify, which meant running a marathon in under 3 hours, 20 minutes. I'd never run anything longer than a half-marathon—and let me tell you, those final 13 miles make the first 13 feel as easy on the body and mind as jogging. *Just like it feels to write the second half of a book.*

I took the plunge. I did everything wrong in my first marathon, running it like a half, going too fast early on, and "bonking," or hitting that proverbial wall, with 10 miles left in the race. *Same thing that happens when bolting out of the blocks too fast with a book that isn't well-planned or thought out.* I was hurting, badly. However, I knew that if I didn't jog, shuffle, walk, limp or crawl past that finish line, I'd never try again to go to Boston. And pride alone prevented me from dropping out of my one and only marathon. So, with great discomfort I instantly feel to this day when closing my eyes and remembering, I got across the line.

A year later, much more familiar with the process of pacing and conserving energy for the long haul, I easily qualified for Boston—a dream come true. Since, I've been four times, and will be closing a racing career full of amazing experiences by running Boston #5 in 2017.

What happened here? How does one terrible race turn into many good races and a dream fulfilled—over and over again?

I learned how to finish. Not coincidentally, in the time since I ran my first Boston in 2005, I have started and finished 20 books (as of the end of 2016). Prior to 2005, I had edited several books, but never finished writing one.

Marathon racing or book writing share a number of noteworthy parallels:

- We start with a vast supply creative, physical and emotional energy, borne by weeks and months (or years) of thinking about our memoir, novel, non-fiction book, or other major piece of writing. We're like thoroughbreds at the starting gate.
- Our first few chapters (miles) feel *great*—we write them with great intensity and energy, getting into the flow, loving the process. *Is this all there is to it?*

- A few chapters further, we come across early obstacles—characters that don't mesh. Details that aren't right. Narrative or plotting problems we can't immediately fix. Situations we either didn't outline or anticipate, or for which we lack the pure writing skill. This equates to the 8- to 12-mile mark of a marathon, when the euphoria of competing wears off, and we're faced with a "monkey mind," spinning over what might go wrong, the little twinge we feel in our legs . . . early obstacles.
- After plowing along, we hit the wall—the story seems to fall flat. We may have written 10 chapters, 15, or even 20, but now, we've "bonked." We're mentally exhausted, out of ideas, and our experiences aren't translating well to narrative. The hardest thing to do is get up and continue writing. This directly parallels "hitting the wall" in marathoning or other extreme endurance sports, when our muscles feed on themselves to draw sustenance. The mind shuts down, the body follows, and the next step feels like walking on fiery coals. But weren't we clipping along nicely a couple miles (chapters) before?
- We gather our deeper forces, our will to finish, our will to succeed . . . *our will to write this complete story.* We reduce our daily goals to something attainable, if necessary. If we were writing 1,000 or 2,000 words a day, we might cut to 500. Our brains and "muses" show us ways to bring the story home. We stop for the day in mid-paragraph, at a particularly hot, dramatic, or exciting passage—and pick up there, to begin with sustained momentum. I always equate this with miles 20-25 of a marathon, when every stride is an effort, and my mind and body now work in concert to get me home, one coaxing the other, one pushing forward, the other shutting off reminders of how far I've already run. *One step at a time. One sentence or paragraph at a time.*
- Suddenly, by shortening our daily expectations and writing sessions if necessary—*by shortening our stride*—we find ourselves on the final chapter. Quick tip: publishers and editors look at how stories start, sustain, and *finish* before buying books. It must finish as strongly, or stronger,

> than it started. For the final time, we muster up the energy that took us through months of preparation, and every chapter leading to this point. Our goal: to finish *strong.* It's not enough to crawl across the line. The picture I have held in my mind on the final chapter of all 20 books is one and the same—running the final 600 meters down Boylston Street in Boston, with more than 150,000 people screaming and cheering. Do I want to just finish? Or do I want to finish? Invariably, a breath of energy comes from somewhere and I finish strong. Nothing like crossing a finish line at full tilt. Which is exactly how we should finish our stories and books.

We entered this journey with a vision, an outline, the fruits of our preparation (voluminous notes, transcripts, character bibles, sketches, and any other "supplies"), and a plan for success. While writing, we made dozens, hundreds, or even thousands of decisions on the fly, adjusting and readjusting to keep our vision aligned with where the story was taking us. We pushed through obstacles, slowed down our pace as necessary, and then pushed one final time, with our fullest physical, emotional, and mental faculties. We finished with a great ending, our very best effort.

If I change ten words above from writing vernacular to running-speak, I will have described how marathons are run. Few life achievements beat the feeling of writing a book, or running 26.2 miles in a few hours (my ultramarathon friends tell me ultras are even more incredible, but they're crazy and I'll take their word for it! 26.2 is enough for me). It stays with you forever, which leads to my final point in this analogy: *Once you finish, it becomes easier to finish again.*

When I'm writing a book, it becomes a central focus of my life. So should yours, taking a place alongside family, significant other, your health (physical, spiritual, emotional, mental), and your day job. It should not receive a lower priority; if it is, chances are, you won't finish. Everything else in my life either supports my writing effort, or it falls by the wayside temporarily. Or permanently. Sound extreme? Walk into your local library or bookstore, and look around. I'll bet my vocabulary that more than 95 percent of the authors of those books gave their projects tip-top priority.

My non-writing friends sometimes can't understand why I don't return calls or e-mails for weeks, or can't see them for four or five months. Some people might think of this as extreme or unbalanced; to the salaried, 9-to-5 world where we support the expectations of others, maybe so. But Joyce Carol Oates, Anne Rice, Jane Smiley, Gillian Flynn, Lois Erdrich, Tom Wolfe, J.K. Rowling, Jim Harrison, Anne Lamott, and even writing machines like Janet Evanovich and James Patterson, do not reach the finish line by picking at their manuscripts as a little side hobby. They dig in, immerse into the creative dream, marry their life experiences to their imaginations, silence the world, and *go.* As George Lucas has said over the years, through interviews, Yoda, and otherwise, the only thing that matters is *doing*—finishing. *There is no try; there is only do.* Lucas made *American Graffiti* in 28 furious days while living on cokes and candy bars; he's not one to embrace excuses from his producers, special effects wizards, actors and cameramen about why a scene or movie didn't come in on schedule.

The most important aspect of finishing is how we practice daily. When we're writing books, it's more important to be consistent than to get caught up in creative peaks and valleys. I can assure you those will happen as the process moves into weeks and months. When I co-wrote *When We Were The Boys* with Stevie Salas, my teen friend who became Rod Stewart's lead guitarist in the late 1980s, we had an immediate challenge: the publisher bumped up production and wanted the manuscript in four months. We hadn't started yet. Then, Stevie's father, whom he revered, took a turn for the worse with lung cancer and passed away. Between the final stages, and the shock of losing his Dad, Stevie was essentially AWOL for two of those four months. The publisher didn't budge on the deadline.

Thankfully, Stevie knew how to write songs in a crunch, and I benefitted from years of daily newspaper deadline writing. Crunch time is crunch time, whether you're on a basketball court or staring down the business side of a deadline. While traveling around the world to fulfill his many music obligations, Stevie wrote overlays on his iPhone, his iPad, backs of napkins—and I expanded them into chapters. We did not come up for air that I know of. We wrote the entire book in six weeks. No choice. We never spent more than six or eight hours a day on the book, until the final week, when we pulled all-nighters. However, we worked nearly all 42 days. We set daily goals and hit them. We sent it in, rough edges and all.

That's exactly what reviewers cited as the strength of the book—its raw edginess, the emotional depth Stevie drew into a book that started as a 22-year-old kid's overnight ride from backyard gigs to sold-out stadiums (every young musician's dream), and turned into a wonderful look at the psyche of rock and roll. In our haste to finish, we didn't have time to *edit and polish the heartbeat out of the story.* He wrote overlays, I turned them into full chapters, we revised once, proofed once—and off it went. Six months later, we were signing copies at a bookstore near you.

Many times, when I'm stuck on a manuscript, I wish again I could bottle and drink that experience like an energy drink.

APPLY & INTEGRATE

This leads to the *real* secret of success, of finishing strongly in all achievements, really: *deliberate practice.* In our case, Stevie had spent 25 years on deadline in recording studios, doing whatever needed to be done in order to finish with a piece that matched his exacting standards. Plus, he'd written over 500 songs, so he knew how to get in and out of stories and anecdotes quickly. I had spent 35 years on journalism and book deadlines, revising and rewriting as much as I wrote original material. That adds up to a lot of hours of specific practice (I'd say 50,000 hours between us, easily) before we joined forces for *When We Were The Boys.*

Look at the experts or masters in any field or endeavor, be it sports, business, community service, teaching Sunday School, or writing a book. They reorder their preparations, and lives, so that virtually everything they do feeds into their next performance or effort. An example: I prepped for writing *When We Were The Boys* by reading up on Stevie and Rod Stewart. Then I bought Stewart's *Out of Order* album, the record for which Stevie toured with him, and I bought some of Stevie's solo work. I listened day and night, getting into the psyches of the two through their music. When we wrote, I made it a point to listen to a Stevie Salas or Rod Stewart song, or watch a YouTube video, *every day.* I also pulled out my journal and sketched out ideas, experimented with ways to write passages, and added follow-up questions to ask. I called Stevie and rapped about music; he's as much a fan as a performer, and we like the same music, so that was fun and easy. All of this falls under *deliberate practice,* where every step feeds the bigger goal and forces the mind to engage completely. Contrast this with a regular practice, in which the mind might wander several times, we might skip or brush over a step to get to the next one, and we'll skip details we deem unimportant. In deliberate practice, every detail is important, no matter how small or seemingly inconsequential.

If you adopt the spirit of deliberate practice in your writing, I guarantee you will not only reach the goal you hold in your head today—but will exceed it, many fold. If ordinary practice is our ticket to success, deliberate practice is the rocket fuel that thrusts us into something beyond our previous expectations.

Earlier, I mentioned something that, if you haven't yet written a book, might have started your heart palpitating: You're not finished after your first draft. You're only just beginning. And, you're not finished after you send in your final draft, or opt for a self-publishing route. You're only just beginning the marketing and promotion phase. I won't elaborate on the latter, as this is a writing process book and there are excellent book marketing and promotion titles on the shelves. However, I will briefly show the final stages of how an idea becomes a final, published work.

Once you've written the first draft and taken a breather, it's time for round two—typically, a full rewrite. *You mean we have to go through the process again?* To be fair, yes. Remember: your one and only goal in first draft is to get the story down. Just get it on paper, and then get to work. New authors often try to line-edit, cut and paste in the second draft. However, with very few exceptions, rewrites are necessary. Why? It takes several writing sessions to nail the rhythm of your narrative, your voice, and the voices of your characters. It usually takes several chapters. Since your first draft of chapter four or five likely is stronger than your first draft of chapter one—you're now fully into the flow—those first chapters need to be rewritten. Once done, you'll see the others need to be rewritten, too, in order to match the cohesiveness and rhythm that you have developed. That's why novelist and memoirist Anne Lamott refers to the first go-rounds as "shitty first drafts." Stephen King advises us to "leave them in the closet." These are masters who have sold millions of books.

You might need to rewrite again. Or, if the narrative is cohesive, the voice strong and all story and plot points solid, you can begin revising. I refer to this as the Michelangelo Phase, taking that solid block of story and chiseling and polishing until every line of your story shines from the inside out. Your manuscript must be on fire from the first sentence. The first five pages mean everything to an editor and agent. The first fifty pages mean everything to a reader. If you can't hook them within 50 pages, you'll lose them. You might have to rewrite those 50 pages, or first few chapters, five or ten times to get them right. As mentioned before, the irony is that in first draft, your first fifty pages are often *the worst part of the manuscript,* because the rhythm of the narrative and rapport with your characters is still being established.

How many rewrites and revises do you need to finish and hit *send? As many as necessary.* A good procedure would be to write your first draft, rewrite completely, make an extensive editing and revision of the rewritten draft, then polish narrative, lines of dialogue, and transitions. Remove anything that seems to be extraneous, wordy or overwritten—"purple prose." Get rid of personal favorite passages that hold up or don't fit with the story—what I call "little darlings." Read your dialogue aloud in the voices of your characters, like a stage actor. Your own ear will let you know what sounds authentic, what sounds contrived.

Rewrite, and rewrite again. Do whatever it takes to get it right.

Once you are truly finished, take a break. Read, nourish, exercise, regenerate. Then circulate your work to agents and editors, or self-publish if that is your aim—and move onto the next writing project before the just-completed work can drag you back in. Enjoy the exhilaration and the sense of accomplishment. You earned it.

EXERCISES

- When you're well into an article, story or book, take the first chapter or first two paragraphs, and rewrite. Save your original draft, and notice the difference. See if you can tell the difference between "starting out" and writing when you've been with the material for some time.

- Take an article, journal entry or story you wrote some time ago. Revise and edit it to a fine polish, in a way that reflects your current skills. Study the changes and why you made them.
- The final assignment: Take a work-in-progress all the way. Finish, edit and polish your work—and start on the next essay, article, novel, memoir or non-fiction work.

QUESTIONS FOR FURTHER DISCOVERY

- What are some of the obstacles and challenges that I face when trying to finish something very important to me? How can I overcome them? What can I change in my daily routine to create a better outcome?
- What are some of the ways in which I can more deeply focus myself during the middle of a major writing project, when I am beyond the emotional high of starting out, yet cannot yet see the "finish line"?
- How can I further focus my non-writing time to keep the flow of my work going? What can I be doing that feeds the book—or feeds my writing?
- Do I have a system of milestones and mini-rewards to propel and motivate me? How can I incorporate them into my writing?
- When I finish a book or article, do I feel relieved? Sad? Happy? Depressed? Ready to sleep? Or ready to embark on the next project?

On that note, I can't wait to read your articles or stories. I am eagerly anticipating the good news about your successes. Give yourself over to writing through your heart and soul, about your life experiences, and you will find success—in yourself, in the publishing world, or even by writing the most heartfelt church newsletter around. If you write a book, I'll be your biggest fan—because I know you've put your life experience into it, and you've achieved something truly tremendous. *Write On!*

BOOKS BY ROBERT YEHLING

From Open Books Press

Writes of Life: Using Personal Experiences in Everything You Write

The Write Time: 366 Exercises to Fulfill Your Writing Life

Fiction

Voices

Turning the Page (2017)

Memoir

Rooting (2017)

Non-Fiction

Creating Adventures, Sharing Stories

Just Add Water: A Surfing Savant's Journey with Asperger's

Beyond ADHD (with Jeff Emmerson)

The Champion's Way (with Dr. Steve Victorson)

When We Were The Boys: Coming of Age with Rod Stewart (with Stevie Salas)

Writing

Shaping, Shifting, Polishing: 50 Premier Self-Editing Strategies (e-book)

Sharing Stores, Creating Adventures: Best of the Word Journeys Blog

Literary: Poetry, Essays, Commentary

Backroad Melodies

Coyotes in Broad Daylight

Open Meadows

The River-Fed Stone

Shades of Green

Edited by Robert Yehling

The Hummingbird Review: Stories, Poems & Essays from New & Established Writers

ABOUT THE WORD JOURNEYS WRITING INSTITUTE

The Word Journeys Writing Institute is an online and onsite clearinghouse of programs, courses and resources dedicated to the best in creative, media, business, and book writing and publishing. It is built upon the two flagship books behind the past 15 years of mentoring, coaching, consulting, editing, teaching and writing in Word Journeys programs, published by Open Books Press: *The Write Time: 366 Exercises to Fulfill Your Writing Life,* and *Writes of Life: Using Personal Experiences in Everything You Write.* A third, *Write Deep Heal Deep,* will be published in 2017.

Writers of all abilities experience a variety of online and onsite courses, workshops, retreats, mentoring, creative and marketing consultation. We work with authors, journalists, publishers, editors and screenwriters from throughout the world. Many will present workshops in The Word Journeys Writing Institute Series.

Modeled after Denver, Colo.'s successful Lighthouse, The Word Journeys Writing Institute features innovative courses and workshops in fiction and narrative non-fiction, sci-fi/fantasy, memoir/autobiography, travelogue, playwriting, screenwriting, marketing and promotion, self-publishing, editing, therapeutic and personal journaling, book and magazine journalism. We also offer specific writing programs tailored to grades 4 and higher, as well as to educational, corporate, and institutional groups.

Headquartered in Southern California, The Word Journeys Writing Institute also offers a variety of tools and resources for working writers. These include the four books in the Word Journeys Writers Series: *The Write Time; Writes of Life; Write Deep Heal Deep;* and *Just Cause: Writing with Purpose* (the latter two to be published in 2017).

The Word Journeys Writing Institute opens in September, 2016. For our upcoming calendar of events, workshops, courses and resources, visit www.wordjourneys.com.

ABOUT THE AUTHOR

Award-winning writer Robert Yehling is the author of 17 works of fiction, non-fiction, poetry and essays, and the ghostwriter of many others. His biography of autistic surf star Clay Marzo, *Just Add Water,* won a 2016 Los Angeles Times Book Prize and was a finalist for the 2015 Dolly Gray Literature Award. He also won an Independent Publishers Book Award for the first edition of *Writes of Life.*

Born in Illinois, Yehling moved to California in the early 1960s. He became a journalist at age 16 in 1976, spending his formative years as a sportswriter, music reviewer, news journalist, and feature writer. He moved on to edit and write for numerous magazines and websites, before focusing primarily on book writing and editing in the 21st century. Yehling has since edited more than 150 books—several of which became bestsellers. He also has won writing awards from the prestigious Society of Professional Journalists in three categories: newspaper, magazine, and online.

Yehling's other love is teaching. Since 1999, he has presented more than 250 workshops and classes on all forms of fiction and non-fiction writing, plus marketing, promotion, and editing. He has taught at writer's conferences, retreats, workshops, college extension programs, middle and high schools, as well as serving as a creative writing professor at Ananda College in Northern California. He continues to guest-teach high school and college classes, both in person and through Skype.

Besides his own books, Yehling is editor of *The Hummingbird Review,* a journal of international poetry, short fiction, and non-fiction writing from new and experienced authors.

Yehling makes his home in Southern California, where he enjoys all ocean sports, hiking, running, gardening, and building dioramas.

OTHER TITLES FROM OPEN BOOKS PRESS

Resting Places | Michael C. White
5-Star review in *Foreword Reviews*

A woman's journey of self-discovery and spiritual awakening

After receiving the devastating news of her son's death, Elizabeth ekes out a lonely and strained relationship with her husband, Zach. While he takes comfort in support groups, Elizabeth becomes withdrawn and seeks solace from the only thing that helps her forget: alcohol. A chance meeting with a man on the side of the road spurs her to travel cross-country to the site of her son's death in the hope of understanding what had happened.

During the trip, she undergoes a transformation, one which allows her to confront the demons of her past but also to acknowledge the possibilities of her future. Through the wisdom and kindness of a man she meets along the way, she finds a means not only of dealing with her pain and her guilt, but of opening herself to the redemptive power of love, and of faith in something. *Resting Places* is an inspiring, upbeat story, a tale of real faith in what we cannot see except with our hearts, a novel that follows a character from despair to hope, from despondency to renewal.

An Incredible Talent for Existing: A Writer's Story | Pamela Jane

It is 1965, the era of love, light—and revolution. While the romantic narrator imagines a bucolic future in an old country house with children running through the dappled sunlight, her husband plots to organize a revolution and fight a guerrilla war in the Catskills.

Their fantasies are on a collision course.

From her vividly evoked existential childhood ("the only way I would know for sure that I existed was if others—lots of others—acknowledged it") to writing her first children's book on a sugar high during a glucose tolerance test, Pamela Jane takes the reader along on a highly entertaining personal, political, and psychological adventure.

Wide as the Wind | Edward Stanton
Fall 2016

The lyrical tale of a boy, a girl, their island, and how they saved it.

Wide as the Wind is the first novel to deal with the stunning, tragic history of Easter Island (Vaitéa). It could be described as quest fiction for all ages in the line of Tolkien's *The Hobbit,* but it is set in the real world, not Middle-earth. *Wide as the Wind* portrays Polynesian voyages across the Pacific Ocean in canoes with no metal parts or instruments: the greatest adventure in human prehistory, as bold as modern space voyages *(National Geographic).*

When Vaitéa is ravaged by war, hunger and destruction, it falls upon Miru, the fifteen-year-old son of a tribal warrior, to sail to a distant island to find the seeds and shoots of trees that could reforest their homeland. If he decides to undertake the voyage, he must leave behind Kenetéa, a young woman from an enemy tribe with whom he has fallen deeply in love. And if Miru and his crew survive the storms, sharks and marauding ships that await them on a journey over uncharted ocean, an even greater mission would lie ahead. They must show their people that devotion to the earth and sea can be as strong as war and hatred. *Wide as the Wind* is both a stirring novel of adventure and a prophetic tale for our times.